NEW EDITION

Better
Writing

**A step-by-step approach
to improving writing skills**

RICHARD HARRISON

Published by
Garnet Publishing Ltd.
8 Southern Court
South Street
Reading RG1 4QS, UK

www.garneteducation.com

This edition first published 2014
ISBN 978-1-78260-121-0

Production

Project manager: Sarah MacBurnie
Editorial: Sarah Whiting, Sue Coll, Alan Dury
Design: Mark Tilley-Watts
Illustration: Doug Nash

Printed and bound in Lebanon by International Press:
interpress@int-press.com

Contents

To the student

How will this course help me?

This course will help you to write better paragraphs in English. 'Better writing' means writing that is:

▶ more accurate ▶ easier to read ▶ appropriate to the reader ▶ more interesting

Why is it important to be accurate?

For most kinds of writing it is important to make sure that spelling, punctuation and grammar are correct. If you make mistakes in speech it doesn't usually matter much, as long as people understand your meaning. But when you write, people expect much more accuracy, especially if you are writing as part of your job (letters, reports, etc.) or as part of your studies (essays, examinations, etc.).

What does 'easier to read' mean?

This means that the writing is more fluent. The sentences are not too short and not too long. They link together neatly so that the meaning in one sentence is carried into the next, and so on. As a result, it is easy for the reader to get the message – to find out what you want to say.

How do I know if my writing is 'appropriate'?

Find out about different writing styles. The way you write to a friend is not the same way that you write to a new boss or the head of a college. Learn about formal and informal language. When you write, imagine the reader. What does he or she expect from your writing? That will also make your writing more interesting!

How can I make my writing 'better'?

1 Go through *Better Writing* and complete all the units. In each unit, the first section ('Looking at text') asks you to look at material other people have written. It picks out language points which are important to understand if you are going to write well, and it gives you exercises to practise that language. The remaining sections of each unit focus on other things which will help you write better. Each unit contains a section on sentence building, ways of joining short sentences together, improving the way you put sentences together to make paragraphs, punctuation, checking (or 'editing') what you have written and building your vocabulary.

2 Reading helps writing, so read as much as you can in English. Read anything that is interesting and not too difficult for you. Try graded readers, newspapers, magazine articles, information on the Internet and even advertisements or airline brochures.

3 When you read, be aware of different styles of English.

Good luck!

What's it like?

A Focus on the sentence

Looking at text

1 Maria, Salah, Yoko and Tony are writing to friends. Read the four paragraphs and match these people with the pictures. Write their names below the pictures.

A Maria is writing a letter to a friend in Singapore.

I've got a new mobile phone. It's quite light and it's small, so it's easy to carry in my pocket. It weighs 140g and it's only 11cm long. It has a back cover to protect it, mine is red. I love it! I can keep in touch with my family and friends all the time. It's got a large, touch screen, so I can text easily, check emails and go online. I use my phone when I go shopping and I take it everywhere, although I have to switch it off at college when I'm in class!

B Salah is sending an email message to a friend in Japan.

My brother bought a jeep a couple of weeks ago. It's in excellent condition, although it's second-hand. I think it's about four years old. It's a Yakono Scorpion with air-conditioning and power steering. It's quite fast, and of course it's got four-wheel drive. My brother uses the car when he goes camping in the desert. The air-conditioning is fantastic. It's also got a roof rack on the top, which is very useful for luggage and water containers. There's also a spare tyre on the back. I hope he'll let me borrow the jeep sometimes!

C Yoko is also sending an email to Habiba, a friend in Jeddah.

I've got a new watch. My cousin gave it to me last week. It's quite attractive, but it's very unusual! It's made of metal and the style is very modern. I think it's French. The face of the watch is square in shape and it's silver with long white hands. It's a very big watch, and the face measures nearly 5cm across! There are no numbers on the face, which is strange. It hasn't got the date on it either. The strap is red and is made of plastic. I think I like the watch, but I'm not sure!

D Tony is writing to a friend in Sweden.

I've got some good news. My brother and I have got a boat! We bought it last week. It's not new, but it's in good condition. I think it looks beautiful sailing through the waves. It's made of fibreglass, so it's very light. There's a mast in the middle with a sail. The boat is about 5m long and the mast is 4m high. It's not very fast, but we're very happy with it. The boat is white and the sail is dark green. Its name is 'Gulf Pearl'. It's quite a good name, don't you think?

2 **Read through the paragraphs again.**

a Underline all the verbs that belong with *got*. For example, in line 1 of Maria's letter *I've got* should be underlined.

b What do you think *'s* and *'ve* mean?

's got = _____   've got = _____

LANGUAGE: *have got/has got*

I **have** got ...	We **have** got ...
You **have** got ...	You **have** got ...
He/She/It **has** got ...	They **have** got ...

Look at these sentences:	**We can also say:**
I **have got** a new watch. (I**'ve got** a new watch.)	I **have** a new watch.
It **has got** four-wheel drive. (It**'s got** four-wheel drive.)	It **has** four-wheel drive.
We **have got** a boat. (We**'ve got** a boat.)	We **have** a boat.

Note: This is more common in North American English.

3 **Write sentences about Salah's brother, Yoko, Tony and his brother, the jeep and the boat. Use *has/have* (got).**

EXAMPLE: *Maria has got a new mobile phone.*

a _____

b _____

c _____

d _____

e _____

LANGUAGE: dimensions

The main dimensions of an object are length, width and height.
We can write about dimensions like this:

The table is 2.3m long.
The table is 2.3m in length.
The length of the table is 2.3m.

 4 **Complete column 2 of the table below.**

Adjective	Noun
long	length
wide	
high	
thick	

5 **Read this paragraph about a famous monument in Kuwait. It is called Kuwait Towers.**

a   What is a monument?

_____

b   Can you think of other famous monuments?

_____

When visitors come to Kuwait, they should take a trip to Kuwait Towers. It is a beautiful and very famous monument situated on the coast road. It consists of three tall, thin towers, which are white in colour. There are also three blue spheres on the towers. The towers are wide at the base, but at the top they come to a point. They look like three space rockets pointing to the stars. The towers are not all the same size. The tallest is 187m high and has two spheres. There is a small sphere near the top and a large sphere near the middle. The next-tallest tower is 147m in height with one sphere. The third tower, the smallest, has not got any spheres. Inside the small sphere on the tallest tower there is a viewing area and a restaurant. When you go up in the lift, you can see the whole of Kuwait. It is a wonderful view. The towers and the spheres are used for storing water.

6 **Look at the four illustrations. Read the paragraph again and answer the question.**

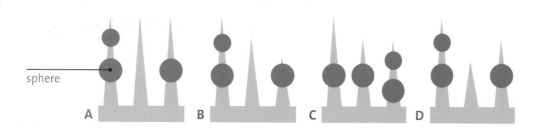

sphere

A   B   C   D

Which illustration shows Kuwait Towers? _____

7   **Now complete the sentences. Write one word in each space.**

a   The monument ___consists___ _____ three towers and three spheres.

b   The towers _____ _____ in colour and the spheres _____ _____ .

c   On the tallest tower, one sphere _____ large and the other _____ _____ .

d   The towers and spheres _____ _____ _____ storing water.

Sentence building

 **8**   **Look at the pictures below. Put these sentences into the table below.
Put the words in the correct order first.**

a   the back / engine / got / has / boat / a small / at / our

b   has / one / each side / on / little radio / speaker / my / got

c   got / the front / have / at / shirts / two pockets / these

d   the right / laptops / have / on / a disk drive / got / many

What?	Verb (*have/has got*)	What?	Where?	.
The jeep	has got	a roof rack	on the top	.
a				
b				
c				
d				

9   **Look at the pictures. Make sentences about each picture and complete the table.**

 red circle   viewfinder   advertisements

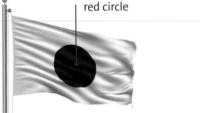  

A the Japanese flag   **B** camera   **C** bus

What?	Verb (*have/has got*)	What?	Where?	.
a				
b				
c				

LANGUAGE: *There is ... , There are ...*

We can also describe things using *there is* and *there are*.

There is a handle on the top of the suitcase.
There are wheels on the bottom.

Find two examples of *there is/are* in the paragraph about Kuwait Towers.
Underline the sentences.

10 Look at the pictures in Exercise 9. Make sentences about each picture using *there* and complete the table.

There?	Verb (*be*)	What?	Where?	.
There	is	a roof rack	on top of the jeep	.
a				
b				
c				

LANGUAGE: *made of/used for*

Look at these sentences. Underline the verbs.	These kinds of verb consist of two parts:
This shirt is made of cotton. These boats are made of fibreglass. The tower is used for storing water. The spheres are used for storing water.	*to be* (*is, are, was*, etc.) + **the past participle form** (*made, used, built*, etc.)

11 Match these things with the materials. Write the sentences in the table.

~~a credit card~~ a knife envelopes tyre metal plastic rubber paper

What?	Verb (*is/are*)	Verb (*made of*)	What?	.
a A credit card				.
b				
c				
d				

What are the items above used for? Choose from the list and write a sentence about each.

sending letters cutting things covering wheels paying for goods and services

What?	Verb (*is/are*)	Verb (*used for*)	What?	.
e A credit card				.
f				
g				
h				

Joining ideas

Look at this sentence:
The watch is red. It has got white hands and a red strap.

We can join it using *with*.

First part of the sentence	*with*	What?
The watch is red	with	white hands and a red strap.

12 **Match these sentences. Use *with* to join the sentences.**

The jeep is new.	It has large, luminous numbers.
The watch is oval.	It has tinted windows and power steering.
The phone is small.	It has a white mast and a red sail.
The boat is green.	It has silver hands and a gold strap.

a The jeep is new with _____

b _____

c _____

d _____

13 **Write a sentence about each of these things. Use *with*.**

My watch   Our house/flat/apartment   The classroom

EXAMPLE: *My mobile is black with a grey cover.*

a _____

b _____

c _____

d _____

When clauses

A clause contains a verb.

... when we go fishing

**But a clause is not a sentence. It is a part of a sentence.
A clause is like a broken down car. It cannot work on its own.
It needs help.**

We use clauses to join ideas.

We use the boat. + We go fishing. = We use the boat **when we go fishing.**

**There are many kinds of clauses.
A clause beginning with *when* is called a *when* clause.**

14 **Look at Maria and Salah's paragraphs on page 1. Find two sentences with *when* clauses. Write them in the table below.**

Who?	Verb	What?	When?	.
We	use	the boat	when we go fishing	.

Underline the verbs in the *when* clauses. For example, *when we go fishing.*

15 **Add *when* clauses to these sentences. Write the sentences on the lines below.**

EXAMPLE: *I always wear my new watch when I go to the university.*

a   I usually take a camera with me.

b   My brother carries water on the roofrack.

c   Mario never uses his mobile phone.

d   Yoko uses her laptop.

a _____

b _____

c _____

d _____

Check your sentences. Underline the verbs in the *when* clauses.

LANGUAGE

Remember that it is also possible to begin a sentence with the *when* clause.

When it rains in Beijing, it is difficult to find a taxi.

---

16 **Find two sentences beginning with *when* clauses in the paragraph about Kuwait Towers on page 3. Write them in the table below.**

When clause	Last part of the sentence
When I go to the university,	I always wear my new watch.

Punctuation

LANGUAGE: contraction

Look: It's got ... = It **has** got ...   BUT   It's very big. = It **is** very big.   It's made ... = It **is** made ...

 17 **Add punctuation and capital letters to this paragraph.**

its got a memory but it hasnt got a brain its rectangular in shape and quite thin it looks like a briefcase and is about the same size its very easy to carry as it is made mostly of plastic and only weighs about 2kg when you open the lid you find a screen and a keyboard inside people use these machines when they are travelling what is it

How many sentences are there? _____ .   What is it? It's a _____ .

B Focus on the paragraph

Better paragraphs

 1 **Look at paragraph A and paragraph B and answer these questions.**

   a How many sentences are there in paragraphs A and B?   A _____   B _____

   b Underline things in paragraph B that are different from paragraph A.

   c Which paragraph do you think is better? _____ Why?

A

I have got a new watch. The new watch was a present from my sister. Her name is Sarah. My sister is always very kind to me. The watch is oval in shape. It has a white face. The strap is black. The watch is waterproof. I go to the beach at weekends. I wear the watch then.

B

I have got a new watch. It was a present from my sister, Sarah. She is always very kind to me. The watch is oval in shape with a white face and a black strap. The watch is waterproof and so I wear it when I go to the beach at weekends.

2 **Complete this paragraph describing a car. Use the words below.**

there   when   when   also   got   it   it   so   ~~and~~   with

I'm thinking of selling my car, which is about six years old. It's a Gazelle, ^a and_____ it's in quite good condition. The colour is grey ^b_____ dark blue stripes along the sides. ^c_____'s got a sunroof and electric windows. I like to open the sunroof ^d_____ the weather is not too hot. The engine is 2 litres, which is average size. Inside the car everything is black. ^e_____ is a CD player and very good air-conditioning. The seats are made of real leather ^f_____ they are very comfortable. It's ^g_____ four new tyres and the spare tyre is ^h_____ in excellent condition. I hope to get about D 2,000 for the car, ⁱ_____ I decide to sell ^j_____ .

3 Complete this paragraph. Use the information in the picture to help you.

There is a very beautiful and unusual statue in Brussels. It's a statue of a ^a _horse_ and rider and is ^b_____ of iron. The base is ^c_____ in shape and measures about 4 metres ^d_____ and 2 metres ^e_____ The ^f_____ of the statue is about 8 metres. It's very heavy and ^g_____ 4 tonnes. ^h_____'s a man on the horse. He's ⁱ_____ a sword in one hand and a ^j_____ in the other.

rider
shield
sword

horse

8m

4m

2m   4m

weight 4 tonnes

Free writing

4 Choose one of these watches. Write a paragraph about it in your notebook.

Use Yoko's paragraph on page 2 as an example.

Show your paragraph to a partner. Ask him or her to say which watch you are describing.

5 Look at this picture of a boat. Write a paragraph in your notebook describing the boat.

mast heights
4.8m and 5.5m

mast

white sail

wood

boat length 8m

weight 125 tonnes

6   Look at the information in the table. It describes a new car. Write a paragraph about the new car for the readers of an automobile magazine. Use your notebook.

Model	Gazelle
Size	5 seater
Engine size	2.5 litres
Maximum speed	160kph
Air-conditioning	✓
Power steering	✓
Made in	Korea
Price	$35,000
Extras	2 years' free service

7   **Think about a monument in the country where you live.**

Write a paragraph in your notebook describing it.

What does it consist of?

How big is it?

What is it made of?

What does it look like?

Is it used for anything?

Use this checklist to edit your writing in Exercises 4–7.

CHECKLIST	EXERCISE			
	4	5	6	7
How many sentences are there?				
How many full stops (.) are there?				
Does every sentence begin with a capital letter?				
Does every sentence have a verb?				
Have you checked your spelling?				
Can you make your writing better?				

Editing

8   **Check the spelling, punctuation and grammar in this puzzle. There are ten mistakes.**

It is got four legs, but it can't walk It has rectangular in shape and there is a leg at each corner. It measure about a metre in haight. the top is 1.8m long and 70cm waide and has a thickness of 4cm. Ours is made for wood, but sometimes they are made of plastic or glas. In our house we keep it in the dining Room.

What is it?   It's a _____ .

9 There are no mistakes in this paragraph, but how can you make it better? Rewrite the paragraph in your notebook. These words will help you:

> he   it   with   and so   when

My friend Hassan has got a new radio. Hassan bought the radio a few days ago. The radio is black. The radio has a red handle. Hassan likes the radio very much. The radio is very light. Hassan can take the radio everywhere. He has a shower. He takes the radio with him.

Vocabulary building

LANGUAGE: describing size

We can use words such as *big* and *small* to describe the size of something.

It's a **big** car. It's a **small** house. The car is **big**. The house is **small**.

We can also add these words: *quite, very, not very*

The car is **very big**. It's a **very big** car.
The house was **quite small**. It's **quite a small** house.

10 Put these words in order. Start with the smallest.

> quite big   small   not very big   very small   quite small

microchip

smartphone

laptop

desktop computer

tablet

Now write a full sentence about each item.

EXAMPLE: *A microchip is very small.*

_____

_____

_____

_____

_____

Use the words and phrases above to write sentences in your notebook about places you know.

EXAMPLE: *My village is not very big.*

LANGUAGE: describing colours

Look: It's **black**. The colour is **black**. It's **black** in colour.

 Complete the colours in the list.

a The sky at night is b_lack_____ .   **b** The walls are w_____ in colour.

c The sea is a bright b_____ .   **d** The colour of the sky that evening was r_____ .

e What a beautiful y_____ dress! **f** If you mix **c** and **e** you get g_____ .

g If you mix **b** and **d** you get p_____ .

LANGUAGE: describing materials

Look: The shirt is made of **cotton**. The **cotton** shirt.

 What materials do you know? Add to this list.

It's made of ...

cotton   silk   metal   plastic   wood   gold   _____   _____

Now write a sentence for each in your notebook.

EXAMPLE: *This shirt is made of cotton.*

LANGUAGE: describing shape

Look: It's **square**. It's **square** in shape. Its shape is **square**.

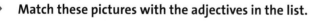 **Match these pictures with the adjectives in the list.**

square   oval   round   ~~rectangular~~   long   thin

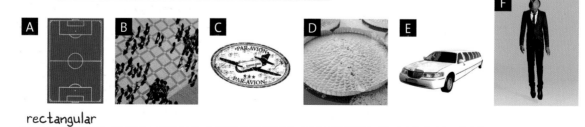

rectangular   _____   _____   _____   _____   _____

LANGUAGE: describing condition

Look: It's in good condition.

14   **Put these words in order in the list below.**

> quite good   ~~excellent~~   very good   not very good   ~~bad~~   good

a It's in <u>bad</u>_____ condition.   **b** It's in _____ condition.

c It's in _____ condition.   **d** It's in _____ condition.

e It's in _____ condition.   **f** It's in <u>excellent</u>_____ condition.

Unit 1 Language review

A Dimensions

1   **Write sentences in your notebook to describe the dimensions of these objects.**

A   **length** 24cm

width 18.5cm

weight 1.05kg

B   **length** 4.83m

height 1.82m   **width** 2.1m

weight 3180kg

2   **Choose an object – a mobile phone, a desk, a laptop, etc. Measure the dimensions (and the weight if you can). Write three sentences about it.**

B *There is/There are*

3   **Look at the flags below. You will need these words:** *stripes, sun, star, crescent, triangle, wheel, sword, dagger.*

Choose two of the flags. Write sentences about them. Use *there is/are*.

There	*is/are*	What?	Where?	.

4 Look at the picture below. Write five sentences in your notebook about the building using *there is/are*.

large windows

balconies

five floors

benches

gardens

public park

C *Made of/Used for*

What?	Verb (*is/are*)	Verb (*made of/used for*)	What?	.
A credit card	is	made of	plastic	.
Envelopes	are	used for	sending letters	.

5 Choose three of these objects. What are they made of? What are they used for?
Write two sentences in your notebook for each.

a calculator

a (supermarket) trolley

suitcases

a ball (football)

bats (baseball, cricket)

tents

mobile phone

a barbecue

D *When* clauses

Who?	Verb	What?	When?	.
I	usually eat	some fruit	when I feel hungry	.

When?	Who	Verb	What?	.
When I feel hungry	I	usually eat	some fruit	.

6 **Put these words in the right order and complete the tables. They all contain *when* clauses.**

a often plays / when / Sami / he has free time / football

b when / we / we go on a picnic / plenty of food / always take

c the exam finishes / the examiner / all the papers / when / collects

Who?	Verb	What?	When?	.
a				
b				
c				

d batteries / must change / when / the / you / the clock stops

e the weather / always use / air-conditioning / we / becomes very hot / when

f usually listens / when / she / to her favourite music / Maria wants to relax

When?	Who?	Verb	What?	.
d				
e				
f				

7 **Complete these sentences in your own words.**

a When it rains in my country _____

b _____ when I am 65.

c When the petrol tank is nearly empty _____

Now add *when* clauses to these sentences.

d I put on my best clothes when _____

e You can see the whole city when _____

f I feel happiest when _____

A Focus on the sentence

Looking at text

1 **Read about mobile phones, then label the diagram below. Use these words:**

mobile switching centre   base station   cell

A MOBILE PHONE

A mobile phone, or cellular (cell) phone, is a very useful appliance. You can use it anywhere – at home, at college, in the street, in a car or even when you are in the desert. When you make a call to a friend, a signal <u>is sent</u> by your phone and collected by a base station. This is a special aerial which is situated on the top of tall buildings or hills.

There are many of these base stations throughout a country or region, and they form a network of 'cells' which cover the whole area. From the base station, the signal is picked up by a mobile switching centre. The signal is then transferred from there to the receiving cell's base station. The second base station can then connect the signal to the receiving mobile phone and you can speak to your friend. Of course, if your friend's phone is outside the range of the network (or switched off!) then you cannot make the call.

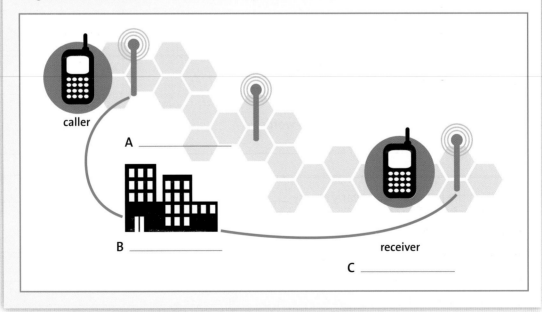

caller

A _____

B _____

receiver

C _____

LANGUAGE: passive verbs

Look at sentences a and b. Underline the verbs.

a The phone sends a signal.   **b** A signal is sent by the phone.

The verb in sentence b is a passive verb. We often use passive verbs when we explain how something (like a mobile phone) works. We form passive verbs like this:

to be	past participle
is	sent
are	connected
was	given
were	taken
must be	passed
can be	opened

2 **Complete the tables with the sentences below. Some have passive verbs and some have active verbs.**

a The kettle heats water.

b Electricity is produced by the sun.

c The washing machine washes clothes.

d The computer must be protected by a password.

e My phone can store 200 numbers.

f Some cars are powered by batteries.

What?	(Active) Verb	What?
The phone	sends	a signal.

What?	(Passive) Verb	By what?
A signal	is sent	by the phone.

3 **Read the paragraph about mobile phones again.**

a Underline all the passive verbs. The first one (*is sent*) has already been done for you.

b There is one *when* clause. Underline it.

c There is also one clause beginning with *if*. Underline it.

d Find *it* in line 1, *This* in line 3 and *there* in line 7. *It* here means a *mobile phone*. What are the meanings of the other two words?

This = _____   there = _____

4 **Read this text about answering machines. Who records the messages?**

a The outgoing message is recorded by _____ .

b The incoming message is left by _____ .

 Staying in touch

It is important to stay in touch with family, friends or our work. However, sometimes we are busy and not able to answer our phone. One way to do this, on a fixed-line phone, is to use an answer machine. It is easy to use.

First of all, someone living in the house has to record a message on the machine. This is called the 'outgoing' message. Usually people say something like – 'Hello. This is Doha 12345. We're not at home at the moment. Please leave a message after the "bleep". When you go out, switch the machine on. When callers phone you, they hear your message and they can then leave a message for you if they want. The 'incoming' messages are recorded onto your machine and stored. A display on the machine shows you how many messages you've got.

When you get home, press the 'play' button and listen to your messages. The messages can be played again and again if necessary.

Most mobile phone networks offer a free 'voicemail' service. Voicemail is very similar to an answer phone. First of all, the owner of the mobile phone has to record a message. This is called the 'outgoing' message. Usually people say something like, 'Hello. You have reached Anna. I can't answer your call at the moment. Please leave a message after the "bleep". If you don't answer your mobile phone or turn it off, when callers phone you, they hear your message and they can then leave a message for you if they want. The 'incoming' messages are recorded onto your voicemail and stored. A display on your mobile phone shows you if you have any voicemail messages. When you call the voicemail service you can listen to your messages.

5 **Read the text again.**

a The passive verb *is called* is underlined. Underline all the other passive verbs in the paragraph.

b There are five *when* clauses. Underline them.

c Write an outgoing message for your phone.

_____

_____

_____

d How do you think 'voicemail' works? Find out and write a few sentences about it in your notebook.

LANGUAGE: instructions

When we describe how something works we often give instructions.
Look at these instructions and underline the verbs.

a Switch on the answering machine when you go out.
b Leave a message after the 'bleep'.
c Press the 'play' button when you want to listen to your messages.

We use the infinitive form of the verb (without *to*) for instructions:

to switch on = **switch on**   to switch off = **switch off**
to start   = **start**   to open   = **open**

6 **Write sentences a, b and c from the language box opposite in the table below.**

Verb	What?	When?
a Switch on		
b		
c		
d		
e		
f		
g		

Now add these sentences to the table.

d Plug in the machine before you begin.

e Check the user's manual when you have a problem.

f Press the delete button after listening to the messages.

g Don't use the machine before you have read the instructions.

7 **Read this paragraph about a juice extractor.**

The Pulpex Juice Extractor

Congratulations on choosing a Pulpex Juice Extractor!

It is made of extra-strong plastic and is guaranteed for five years. A juice extractor is a healthy way of enjoying fruit and vegetables. This is how it works. First of all, the fruit and vegetables must be washed carefully under a tap. They should then be peeled (if necessary) and cut into small pieces. The machine is then switched on and the pieces are pushed carefully into the feed tube using the pusher (do not use your fingers!). As the machine spins around, juice is separated from the pulp. The juice flows from the outlet in the pulp collector and is collected in the juice jug.

8 **Look at the paragraph in Exercise 7 again.**

a Underline the passive verbs.

b Put the diagrams below in order by numbering them 1–6.

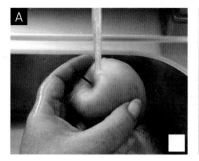
A

B

C

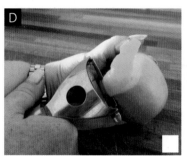
D

E

F

c Now write these past participles under the pictures:

~~collected~~ washed cut switched on pushed peeled

collected

9 **Read the last part of the text about the juice extractor.**

If the pulp container becomes full, switch off the machine, remove the lid and clean out the container. Finally, in order to enjoy a delicious drink full of vitamins, remove the jug and pour the juice into glasses.

a Underline the *if* clause.

b Underline the phrase beginning with *in order to*.

c Find four instructions and write them in the table below.

Verb	What?
Switch off	the machine.

Sentence building

 10 These sentences all have passive verbs. First put the words in the correct order and then write them in the table below. They describe how an MP3 player works.

a folder / the / is / opened / MP3 player / on / the / PC

b copied / the / PC / from / is / music / MP3 player / onto / the

c removed / the / PC / from / MP3 player / is / the

d the MP3 player / headphones / are fitted / the / to

e are / over / the / the / ears / placed / headphones

f pressed / the / is / button / 'play'

g can / as required / the / be / volume / adjusted

What?	Passive verb	How?, Where?, When?	.
The MP3 player	is connected	to the PC	.
a			
b			
c			
d			
e			
f			
g			

 11 Rewrite the sentences above as instructions in your notebook.

EXAMPLE: *Remove the lid from the battery compartment.*

12 Look at these pictures. Write a sentence in your notebook about each picture using a passive verb. Use the verb shown.

EXAMPLE: *Food is stored in a refrigerator.*

store

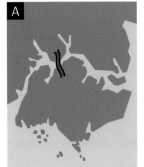

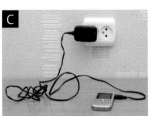

link   plant   connect   open

Joining ideas

LANGUAGE: joining passive sentences

We can join two passive sentences in this way:

The fruit and vegetables are washed. They are cleaned.
The fruit and vegetables are washed and cleaned.

The machine is switched off. The pulp is removed.
The machine is switched off and the pulp removed.

 Join these passive sentences.

a The vegetables are peeled. They are cut into small pieces.
The vegetables are peeled and cut into small pieces.

b The signal is sent to an aerial. It is then transmitted to a telephone exchange.

_____

c The phone is made of plastic. The case is made of leather.

_____

d The outgoing message is recorded. The machine is switched on.

_____

e The juice is poured into a jug. The juice is stored in a refrigerator.

_____

f The clothes are taken out of the machine when the cycle is finished. They are put outside to dry.

_____

LANGUAGE: *as* clauses (time)

To show that two things are happening at the same time we can use an *as* clause of time.

When (*As ...*)	Last part of the sentence	.
As you speak into the answering machine,	your voice is recorded	.
		.

---

14 **Find another example of a sentence with an *as* clause in the paragraph about the juice extractor on page 19. Write it in the table above.**

15 **Match the *as* clauses with the sentences in the table below. Write the full sentence next to the correct picture on page 23.**

When (*As ...*) clause	Last part of the sentence
As climbers go higher up the mountain, ...	clouds form and rain may fall.
As the hurricane gets close to land, ...	vegetation and houses may be destroyed.
As the air rises over the hills, ...	the amount of oxygen in the air decreases.
As the hot lava flows down the volcano, ...	large waves may form.

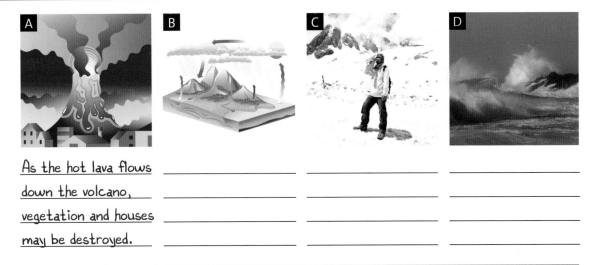

As the hot lava flows
down the volcano,
vegetation and houses
may be destroyed.

LANGUAGE: *if* clauses

An *if* clause tells us about a possibility.

If ...	Last part of the sentence	.
If you want to listen to the message,	press the 'play' button	.

Note: *If* and *as* clauses can be added to the beginning or the end of a sentence.

---

16 Find another example of a sentence with an *if* clause in the paragraph about mobile phones on page 16. Write it in the table above.

17 Match the *if* clauses with the sentences in the table below. Write the full sentence next to the correct picture.

If clause	Last part of the sentence
If the fire alarm sounds, ...	please call our helpline to speak to a computer engineer.
If you have no Internet connection, ...	they should be removed and replaced with new ones.
If the car overheats, ...	staff must use the stairs to leave the building and not the lift.
If the trees start to die, ...	wait for the engine to cool and then add water.

If the trees start to
die, they should be
removed and replaced
with new ones.

18 **Add clauses to these sentences. Remember that the clause must contain a verb.**

a As customers <u>enter the building</u> _____ , they are filmed by video cameras.

b Please remember to lock the door if you _____ .

c If passengers _____ , they should go to the
Lufthansa offices.

d As passengers _____ , they must show their tickets.

e If you _____ , you should see a doctor.

f Please switch off your mobile phone as _____ .

LANGUAGE: *in order to ...*

We use *in order to* + verb (or just *to* + verb) to tell us what something is for.

In order to open the package, cut the corner with a knife.
(To open the package, cut the corner with a knife.)

You must enter your password **in order** to make an online purchase.
(You must enter your password to make an online purchase.)

In order to protect the tablet computer, a cover is included.
To protect the tablet computer, a cover is included.

---

19 **Match these parts of sentences. Then write the sentences in the table below.**

In order to make a phone call,   ... the amount of light must be measured.

To clean pulp from the extractor,   ... speak into the microphone.

In order to record the outgoing message,   ... the required number is keyed in.

To take good photographs,   ... the lid must be removed.

What for? (*In order to ...*)	Last part of the sentence	.
In order to start the machine,	turn the control to number 1 or 2	.
To clean the machine,	the power must be switched off	.

Punctuation

Apostrophes

 20 **What is the difference between these sentences?**

a The student's books are on the desk.

b The students' books are on the desk.

What is the difference between these sentences? Write them out in full.

c The secretary's ill. _____

d The secretary's got a fever. _____

21 **Add apostrophes where they are needed. Some sentences do not need any changes.**

a The dogs got some bad cuts on its leg.

b Im afraid the radios broken.

c The girls are studying Physics and Economics.

d Its situated at the top of a hill.

e Theres a flag at the top of the building.

f Messages are sent by computers.

g The machines switched off at the moment.

h Five teachers have their desks in this room. Its called the teachers room.

Clauses

22 **Find the clauses in these sentences. Add a comma if one is needed.**

a If the caller is in an underground car park it may be impossible to use the mobile phone.

b When the phone is engaged messages can be recorded on voicemail.

c In order to avoid damage to the machine stones must be removed from fruit.

d Contact your local dealer if you have problems with your new television.

e As the door closes the light inside the refrigerator goes off.

f In order to keep a DVD in good condition it should be kept in its case.

g When someone leaves a message on the answering machine a number appears on the display panel.

h The juice is separated from the pulp as the fruit is pushed into the feed tube.

B Focus on the paragraph

Better paragraphs

1 **Read this paragraph about a hairdryer.**

The Superdry hairdryer

The Superdry hairdryer is easy to use and very light in weight. The dryer has a very powerful motor which draws air into the machine and forces it out through a specially designed nozzle. ᵃ As air is drawn into the dryer it passes over the electric heater. The hot air is then forced out. There are two speeds and three levels of heat – warm, hot and very hot. First of all, ᵇ_____ make sure your hands are dry. Select the speed and heat settings you want by turning the arrow. For example, ᶜ_____ , number three should be selected. Hold the dryer about 10cm from your hair and switch the machine on. ᵈ_____ use your styling brush to style your hair. Finally, ᵉ_____ switch the machine off.

Add these five clauses to the paragraph in positions a–e.

when your hair is dry ...	in order to avoid electrocution ...
as you move the dryer over your hair ...	~~as air is drawn into the dryer~~ ...
if you want maximum heat ...	

2 **Complete this passage about a solar cooker. Use the words and phrases in this list.**

is placed   in order to   if   ~~is used for~~   are reflected   avoid
when   begins   and so   must be turned   consists of

A solar cooker ᵃ is used for _____ cooking in dry, sunny countries. It is particularly useful in countries where fuel is expensive. It ᵇ_____ a curved mirror with a stand fixed to the middle of the mirror. The cooker is set up in an open space facing the sun. The mirror is curved, ᶜ_____ the sun's rays ᵈ_____ by the mirror and concentrated onto the stand. ᵉ_____ a pan containing water ᶠ_____ on the stand, it becomes hot. As the pot gets hotter and hotter, the water ᵍ_____ to boil. ʰ_____ get maximum heat, the mirror ⁱ_____ from time to time so that it continues to face the sun. ʲ_____ the food is ready, the pan must be removed carefully. To ᵏ_____ getting burnt while removing the pan, the cook must make sure the mirror is not facing the sun.

3 Read these sentences about a camera. Put them in the correct order and write the paragraph in full in your notebook. (The first sentence has been done for you.)

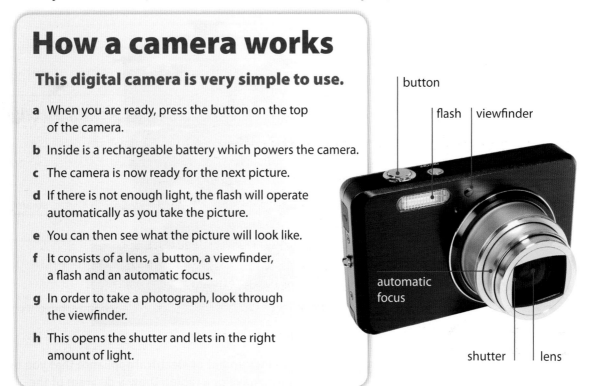

How a camera works

This digital camera is very simple to use.

a When you are ready, press the button on the top of the camera.

b Inside is a rechargeable battery which powers the camera.

c The camera is now ready for the next picture.

d If there is not enough light, the flash will operate automatically as you take the picture.

e You can then see what the picture will look like.

f It consists of a lens, a button, a viewfinder, a flash and an automatic focus.

g In order to take a photograph, look through the viewfinder.

h This opens the shutter and lets in the right amount of light.

button

flash viewfinder

automatic focus

shutter lens

This digital camera is very simple to use.

4 Look through the paragraph you have written in Exercise 3. Find and underline:

a *when* clause   an *if* clause   an *as* clause   the phrase *in order to*

Free writing

5 Read the paragraph about mobile phones on page 16 again. Now look at the diagram below. Explain what happens when you phone someone with a mobile phone from a landline. Use your notebook.

6 Look at this picture of a steamer. Write a paragraph in your notebook, explaining how it is used to cook food. These questions will help you:

What does the steamer consist of?

Where do you put the steamer?

Where does the water go?

Where does the food go?

How does it cook the food?

lid

food

steamer holes

water

work surface

 7 Write a paragraph in your notebook about an instrument or electrical appliance that you own – for example a calculator, an alarm clock, a microwave or a tablet. Draw a diagram of the instrument and explain what it consists of and how it works. When you have finished, show it to someone else in the class to read.

Use this checklist to edit your writing in Exercises 3 and 5–7.

CHECKLIST	EXERCISE			
	3	5	6	7
How many sentences are there?				
How many full stops (.) are there?				
Does every sentence begin with a capital letter?				
Does every sentence have a verb?				
Have you checked your spelling?				
Can you make your writing better?				

Editing

8 Check this paragraph for spelling, punctuation and capital letters. There are ten mistakes. Write the corrected paragraph in full in your notebook.

water-wheels are a very old form of water power They can be maid of wood or metal. They are found in many countrys of the world. There are 17 wooden water-wheels, called 'nurias', in the city of Hama in syria. Water-wheels are usualy located on fast-flowing river's or streams. as the river flows the wheel is turned by the power of the water. The power as used to take watre from the river for farming.

9 There are ten grammatical mistakes in this paragraph. Underline the mistakes and correct them. Then write the paragraph out in full in your notebook.

A computer it is a very powerful instrument. Some computers are heavy and is placed on desks. Other computers are quite small and can carried in the pocket. A computer have many different uses. Information are given to the computer and a set of instructions, called a programme. The computer is tell what to do by the programme. A computer is consists of a monitor with a screen, a keyboard, a disk drive, speakers and a mouse. The keyboard and the mouse are using for getting information into the computer. The 'output' it is shown on computer screen.

Vocabulary building

Instruction verbs

10 Match the instruction verbs with the drawings.

press   push   wait   ~~switch off~~   remove   listen   lift   cut

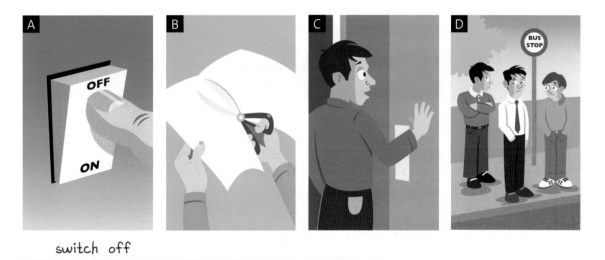

A

switch off

B

C

D

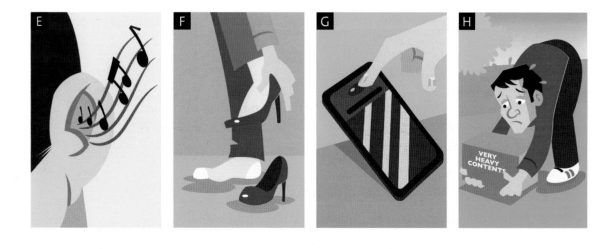

E

F

G

H

Parts of an instrument

 Label the parts of a computer. Use these words:

> screen monitor keyboard mouse printer/scanner

Unit 2 Language review

A Passive verbs

1 Remember, passive verbs consist of two parts:

to be	past participle
is	sent
are	given
must be	connected
can be	passed

Rewrite these active sentences in a passive form. Put them in the table.
Often the agent (*by ...*) is not needed.

a The remote control changes the TV channel.

b The steamer cooks the vegetables.

c I can use my mobile to download music.

d Bridges connect the European and Asian sides of Istanbul.

e Students must not use the lift when there is a fire.

f We use a Sat Nav to give directions.

What?	(Passive) Verb	By what? (agent)	Why? Where? When?
a			
b			
c			to download music.
d			
e			when there is a fire.
f			to give directions.

2 Use the pictures and verbs underneath to write sentences in the present passive in your notebook. Use *is/are/can be/must be*.

mobile phone   paper   ignition   hot water   coffee

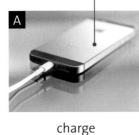      

key

charge   add   put   mix

B Joining passive sentences

> The fruit and vegetables are washed. They are cleaned. They are cut into pieces.

> The fruit and vegetables are washed, cleaned and cut into pieces.

3 Join these sentences in the same way.

a Digital photos can be transferred to a computer. They can be sorted into groups.

_____

b The ice trays are filled with water. They are placed carefully into the freezer compartment.

_____

c At the carwash, cars are washed by machine. They are dried with hot air. Finally they are polished by hand.

_____

C *As clauses*

When (*As ...*) clause	Last part of sentence
As you speak into the answer machine ...	your voice is recorded.

Or ...

First part of sentence	When (*As ...*) clause
Large waves may form ...	as the hurricane gets close to land.

Put these words in the right order and complete the tables.
They all contain *as* clauses.

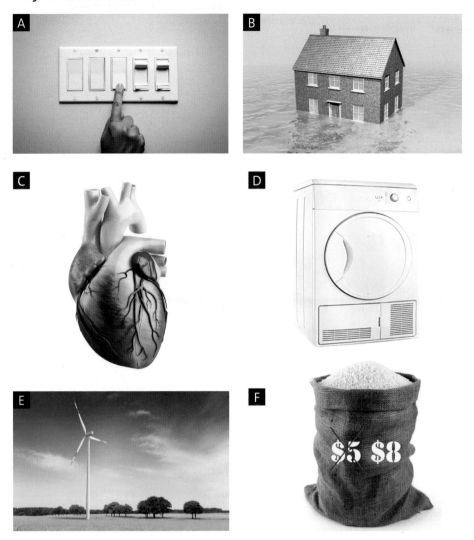

a you leave / lights / as / switch off / the / please / the room

b increases / the sea level / global warming / as / may rise

c around / is pumped / the heart / beats / blood / as / the body

d the dryer / water / from the clothes / as / is extracted / spins

e is produced / of the wind turbine / the wind / the blades / as / turns / electricity

f food / increases / more expensive / the population / will probably become / as / of the world

When (*As ...*) clause	Last part of the sentence
a	
b	
c	

First part of the sentence	When (*As ...*) clause
d	
e	
f	

5   **Write sentences about these pictures using *as*.**

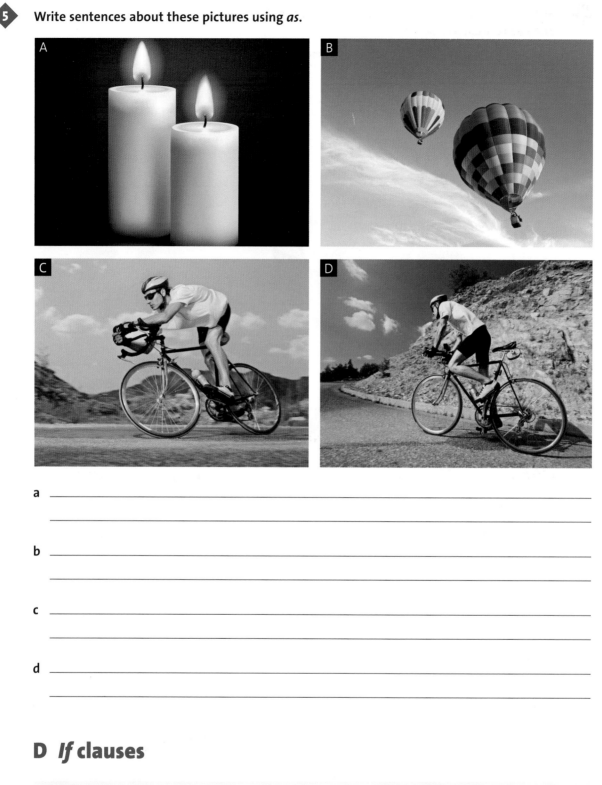

a _____

_____

b _____

_____

c _____

_____

d _____

_____

D *If* clauses

If clause	Last part of sentence
If you want to listen to the message	press the 'play' button.

Or ...

First part of sentence	*If* clause
Please call our helpline to speak to a computer engineer	if you have no Internet connection.

6 Put these sentences in the right order and complete the tables.
They all contain *if* clauses.

a the battery / is fully charged / stops working / the camera / if / check / that

b immediately / an earthquake / everyone / must leave / if / there is / the building

c breaks down / call / your car / the emergency number / if / on the road

d to die / must be / the plants / if / the amount of water / increased / start

e try moving / on your mobile / of your house / no signal / you have / if / to another part

f if / their heart rate / people / exercise / every day / should decrease

If clause	Last part of the sentence
a	
b	
c	

First part of the sentence	*If* clause
d	
e	
f	

7 Write sentences about these pictures using *If*.

a _____

b _____

c _____

E *In order to*

What for? (*In order to*)	Last part of sentence
In order to start the machine (To start the machine)	turn the control to number 1 or 2.

Or

First part of sentence	What for? (*In order to*)
Turn the control to number 1 or 2	in order to start the machine. (to start the machine)

8   **Match the parts of the sentences and write them on the lines below. The first is done as an example.**

a Avoid strong sunlight

b Shut down your computer at night

c Clean the juice extractor carefully after use

d Cars should be polished regularly

e A mobile phone operator must have a good network

in order to

f Exercise, rest and a good diet are required

g Important messages should be saved

save electricity

get the best pictures   avoid blockages

protect the paintwork

provide a strong signal for its users

keep the body healthy

listen to them again

a Avoid strong sunlight in order to get the best pictures.

b _____

c _____

d _____

e _____

f _____

g _____

9   **Complete these sentences in your own words. Use *in order to* ... .**

a I bought a new dictionary _____

b Always store fruit in the fridge _____

c A new motorway is planned _____

d DVDs should be kept in their covers _____

e Avoid watching TV before going to bed _____

f Drink plenty of water _____

A Focus on the sentence

Looking at text

1 **Read this paragraph about how hummus is made.**

HUMMUS

Hummus is a very popular dish in the Arab world. It <u>is made</u> from chickpeas and tahini (sesame seed) paste and it is very easy to make. (First of all), the chickpeas <u>must be soaked</u> for several hours. Then they <u>are drained</u> and placed in a pressure cooker. They are covered with water and a teaspoon of bicarbonate of soda is added. The chickpeas are steamed for about 20 minutes until they are soft. They are then drained and the juice is kept on one side. A few chickpeas should also be kept in order to decorate the dish later on. Meanwhile, the rest of the peas are put into a blender until a soft paste is formed. As the chickpeas are mixed, salt, crushed garlic and tahini paste are all added. After that, a lemon is squeezed and the juice is added to the mixture. The mixture is now soft and creamy.

In order to serve the hummus, the mixture is poured into a dish. Olive oil is added and the extra chickpeas are placed on top. Finally, chopped parsley can be added as decoration around the edge of the dish. Hummus is usually served at room temperature with hot bread. It's delicious!

Put the pictures below in the correct order by numbering them 1–6. Then write these past participles under the correct pictures.

poured   drained   soaked   ~~steamed~~   served   mixed

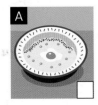

A ☐   B ☐   C ☐   D ☐   E ☐   F ☐

_____ steamed _____ _____ _____ _____

Look at the paragraph on page 37 again. Underline all the passive verbs. Remember that passive verbs have two parts. The first three passive verbs are already underlined.

to be	Past participle
is	made
must be	soaked
are	drained

 Write the passive verbs from Exercise 2 in the correct columns below.

is + past participle	*are* + past participle	modal (*can be*, *must be*, etc.) + past participle
is made	are drained	must be soaked

LANGUAGE: sequence words

When we describe how something is made we use sequence words and phrases such as:

| first | first of all | then | now | next | meanwhile | after that | lastly | finally |

These words tell us the order (or sequence) in which the steps happen.

First, water is heated to boiling point.
Salt is **then** added and stirred.
After that the heat is reduced and ...

4 **Circle the sequence words in the text about hummus on page 37. Write them below.**

First of all

Find the following in the text. Write them on the lines below.

two *until* clauses:

_____

_____

one *as* clause:

_____

two examples of *in order to*:

_____

_____

5 Read this passage about building roads.

HOW
TO BUILD
A ROAD

How do engineers build roads through mountains? Roads such as the Irohazaka Road in Japan give travellers wonderful views but present road engineers with huge problems. This road, which is named after a poem, goes from Tokyo to Kegon Waterfalls. It cuts through high mountains, which are over 1500m in places and has a total of 48 sharp 'hairpin' bends. It is a marvellous engineering project. But where do road engineers begin with such construction?

First of all, a lot of planning is required. Surveys and aerial photos are used in order to choose the best route for the road. Then the route is marked out on the ground by the surveyors. Earth-moving machines are then used to make the route as flat as possible. Cuttings are made through the sides of hills and mountains. Valleys are filled with rock and earth. Bridges and tunnels may also be needed, which of course increases the cost of the project.

When the route is ready, the foundations of the road can be laid using crushed rock. After that a layer of concrete is put on top of the foundations. A machine called a spreader then adds the top surface layer, which consists of concrete or asphalt. Lastly road markings must be painted on the surface and road signs added.

When the road is ready it is opened officially and it can be used by motorists. Many people will drive along these wonderful mountain roads. But how many of these people think about all the planning and hard work that made these roads possible?

a Circle the sequence words.

b Underline the passive verbs. Write them in the table below.

is + past participle	*are* + past participle	modal (*can be, must be*, etc.) + past participle
is required	are used	may be needed

c What are surveys and aerial photos used for?

_____

d Who marks the route out?

_____

e When can the foundations of the road be laid?

_____

f What are added to the road at the end?

_____

LANGUAGE: *by* **after a passive verb**

Look at these sentences:

a The route is marked out **by** the surveyors.
   The road is used **by** many people.
   The sun's rays are reflected **by** the mirrors.

b Hummus is made **by mixing** chickpeas with salt, garlic and tahini.
   First, the road is prepared **by making** the route as flat as possible.
   The peas are softened **by soaking** in water for several hours.

a *By* after a passive verb can tell us **who** or **what** does something.
   FOR EXAMPLE: *the surveyors, many people, the mirrors.*

b *By* can also tell us **how** something is done.
   FOR EXAMPLE: *by mixing, by making, by soaking.*

---

6 Read about the production of perfume at home. Number the pictures below 1–6 to show the steps.

HOW TO MAKE PERFUME AT HOME

Everyone likes perfume, although it is rather expensive to buy in shops. But perfume can also be made at home for very little cost, simply by heating a mixture of flowers and water.

The following items are needed: a bowl, some cheesecloth, fragrant flowers (or blossoms), two cups of spring water (or distilled water), a plate and a saucepan. Some very small perfume bottles are also required.

First the cheesecloth, which is cloth with very small holes in it, is fitted inside the bowl. The flowers are washed and chopped into small pieces. One cup of chopped flowers is placed inside the cheesecloth. The spring water is then poured into the bowl and mixed with the flowers. The bowl is then covered with a plate and left overnight in order to allow the fragrant flowers to soak into the water.

Next, the cheesecloth containing the flowers is carefully lifted from the bowl. All of the liquid should be removed from the flowers by squeezing the cheesecloth. Fragrant water now remains in the bowl. This liquid is poured into a saucepan and heated until it is simmering. It must not boil because this will reduce the fragrance of the perfume. As the water simmers, the quantity of liquid is reduced. The fragrance is made stronger by reducing the quantity. When there is only a little liquid in the saucepan, the heat is removed. The liquid should then be allowed to cool for some time.

When the liquid is completely cool, it is then poured carefully into the perfume bottles. The bottles can then be labelled and given a name. They make perfect presents!

Complete these sentences with phrases using *by ... ~ing* **from the text.**

a Perfume can be made at home

_____

b All of the liquid is removed from the flowers

_____

c The fragrance is made stronger

_____

 Now answer these questions in full sentences. Use the words in brackets in your answer.

a Why is the bowl covered and left overnight? (in order to)

_____

_____

b For how long is the mixture in the saucepan simmered? (until)

_____

_____

c When is the quantity of liquid reduced? (as)

_____

_____

d When is the heat removed? (when)

_____

_____

e When is the liquid poured into bottles? (when)

_____

_____

Sentence building

9 **Add these passive sentences to the table. Put them in the correct order first. They all contain the form** *by ... ~ing*.

a made / tahini paste / together / is / chickpeas / hummus / mixing / and / by

b speaking / the microphone / recorded / into / a message / is / by

c are / seatbelts / wearing / drivers / their / protected / by

d the / saucepan / heating / a / concentrated / in / the / is / by / liquid

e can / to / an eReader / connecting it / charged / be / a computer / by

What?	(Passive) Verb	How?
The flowers	are prepared	by washing and chopping into small pieces.
a		
b		
c		
d		
e		

10 Complete these sentences using *by ...~ing*.

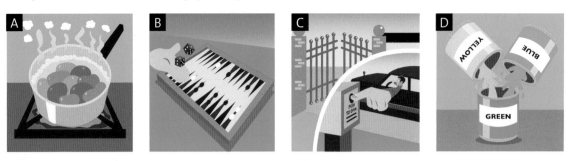

a The potatoes are softened by boiling in a pan of water.

b In backgammon, the pieces are moved by _____

c The gates are opened automatically by _____

d The colour green is made by _____

Now answer these questions in sentences using *by ...~ing* with a passive verb.

e How are channels changed on a TV?

_____

f How is the colour pink produced?

_____

g How can a new language be learned?

_____

LANGUAGE: *also*

***Also* is only a small word, but it is an important way of joining ideas.**
Look at the position of *also* in these sentences.

Hummus is popular in the Arab World. It is **also** popular in Greece and Turkey.
Perfume is produced in factories. It can **also** be made at home.
Maria studies IT at university. She **also** studies Business Administration.

***Now* complete the rule with *before* and *after*.**

Also comes _____ the verb *to be* (e.g., *is*) and modals (e.g., *can*). It comes _____
the main verb.

---

11 Write out these sentences in your notebook. Add *also* to the second sentence.

EXAMPLE: *Hammour is a popular fish in the Gulf States. It is found in other parts of the world.*

Hammour is a popular fish in the Gulf states. It is also found in other parts
of the world.

a Rubber trees are grown in plantations in Southeast Asia. They grow naturally in the Amazon region of Brazil.

b The cursor is moved around the computer screen by using the arrows on the keyboard. It can be moved by clicking the mouse.

c Angelina Jolie is a famous film star. She does a lot of important work for the United Nations.

d Fresh water springs are popular picnic spots. They are an important source of water for some villages.

e The laptop must be switched off at night. The cover should be closed to keep dust from the screen.

12 Write sentences with *also* for each of the sentences below.

EXAMPLE: *Shark meat is sold in fish markets. It can **also** be bought in some supermarkets.*

a My sister likes reading poetry. She _____

b Beijing is an important business centre. It _____

c Qatar Airways flies all over the Middle East. It _____

d Coconuts are grown in the Caribbean. They _____

e Oil is used for manufacturing plastics. It _____

f We can get the news by buying a newspaper in a shop. However, we _____

LANGUAGE: *which* clauses

Look at these sentences:
The road cuts through high mountains.
The road is named after the poem.

We can join these two ideas using a *which* clause.

What?	*Which* clause	Verb + ...
a The road,	which is named after a poem,	cuts through rocky mountains.

A *which* clause can also be at the end of a sentence.

What?	Verb + ...	*Which* clause
b The road	cuts through high mountains,	which are over 1,000m high in places.

Note that *which* refers to the nearest noun.

In a *which* refers to *road*. In b *which* refers to *mountains*. Look:

The **road**, **which** is named after a poem, cuts through high *mountains*. ✓
The road cuts through *mountains*, **which** are over 1,500m in places. ✓
The **road** cuts through mountains, **which** is named after a poem. ✗

---

13 Put these words and phrases in the correct order. Add them to the tables below.
Remember to add punctuation.

a in the west of the country / is located / which / Kuala Lumpur / is the capital of Malaysia

b is popular with both Spaniards and tourists / which / the Spanish dish paella / consists mainly of rice and seafood

What	*Which* clause	Verb + ...
a		
b		

c the largest gold deposits / in South Africa / is mined / which has / gold / in the world

d which is / cashew nuts / a beautiful state in the south of India / are grown / in Kerala

What	Verb + ...	*Which* clause
c		
d		

Find *which* clauses in these paragraphs and underline them.

a Unit 1, pages 1–2, the paragraphs by Salah and Yoko.

b Unit 1, page 3, the paragraph about Kuwait Towers.

c Unit 2, page 16, 'A mobile phone'.

d Unit 3, pages 39 and 40, 'How to build a road' and 'How to make perfume at home'.

How many *which* clauses did you find? _____

Join these sentences using *which* clauses. Write the new sentences in your notebook. Follow this pattern:

What?	*Which* clause	Verb + ...

a Kuwait has a population of more than one million. Kuwait is situated in the north of the Gulf.

   <u>Kuwait, which is situated in the north of the Gulf, has a population of more than one million.</u>

b Bananas are grown in tropical countries such as the Philippines. Bananas need a hot, humid climate.

c The King Faisal Causeway is 24 miles long. It connects Saudi Arabia and Bahrain.

d A scanner is an important part of a modern office. A scanner works by making a digital copy of a document.

e The rababa is made of goat skin stretched over a wooden frame. It is a kind of one-string violin.

Join these sentences using *which* clauses. Write the new sentences in your notebook. Follow this pattern:

What?	Verb + ...	*Which* clause

a An answering machine records messages. The messages can then be played back when you get home.

   <u>An answering machine records messages, which can then be played back when you get home.</u>

b My brother has just bought a Land Rover. A Land Rover is one of the most popular four-wheel-drive vehicles in the Gulf.

c Last week we visited Petra. Petra is the most famous historical site in Jordan.

d The surface of the road is then sprayed with asphalt. Asphalt is a dark, sticky substance produced from petroleum.

e Strips of rubber are passed through rollers. The rollers flatten the strips and produce thin sheets.

LANGUAGE: *although* **clauses**

$$x = \frac{b+b - 4ac}{2a}$$

Although Gunter is a professor of Physics,   ... he doesn't know how to boil an egg.

Although **clauses can go at the beginning or the end of a sentence. Note the position of the commas.**

Although clause	Last part of the sentence
Although Gunter is a professor of Physics,	he doesn't know how to boil an egg.
First part of the sentence	***Although*** **clause**
Gunter doesn't know how to boil an egg,	although he is a professor of Physics.

 17 **Find and underline** *although* **clauses in these paragraphs. Write them in your notebook.**

   a Unit 1 page 1, the paragraphs by Maria and Salah.

   b This unit page 40, 'How to make perfume at home'.

18 **Match the** *although* **clauses with the main sentences. Write out the complete sentences in your notebook. Remember the commas!**

   a Although fishermen have the money to buy modern boats

   b Although the car is eight years old

   c Although Egypt has very low rainfall

   d Although the computer is quite powerful

   e Although it can be very cold in Hong Kong in the winter

   f Although those watches are very cheap

   g Although some perfumes are made in India

... the modem is rather slow.

... it never snows.

... most are imported from France.

... they often prefer to use the old wooden ones.

... many crops can be grown using irrigation.

... it is in excellent condition.

... they are also very attractive.

Although fishermen have the money to buy modern boats, they often prefer to use the old wooden ones.

19 **Write two more sentences about yourself or your city in your notebook.**

Punctuation

 20 **Punctuate these sentences. They all contain** *which* **or** *although* **clauses.**

   a although the suitcase is very large it only weighs 6kg

   b baghdad which is the capital of iraq is situated on the river tigris

   c jemila sends email messages all the time although she found computers difficult to use at first

   d last summer we flew to singapore on qantas which is an australian airline

   e although toyota is a japanese company toyota cars are built in many different countries

   f the dubai shopping festival which takes place in march every year attracts thousands of visitors from all over the region

   g a juice extractor can be used for most types of fruit and vegetables although it is not very suitable for oranges and lemons

B Focus on the paragraph

Better paragraphs

1 Read this paragraph describing how to make *blinis.*

This is a recipe for blinis. They are quite easy to prepare and very filling. (1) About 140g of buckwheat flour is measured and poured into a bowl. Baking powder, salt and an egg are (2) added and mixed together. (3) About 150ml of milk and 3 tablespoons of yoghurt are added and beaten into the mixture. The mixture is (4) left on one side for a few minutes. (5) Heat a little butter in a large pan. Add a tablespoon of the mixture. When the blini is brown on the bottom, it should be turned over and cooked for another minute. The blinis must be kept warn until they are all ready. (6) Serve the blinis. Most people prefer to eat them with sour cream and caviar.

a Add these sequence words to the paragraph by matching them with positions 1–6.

☐ also   ☐ also   ☐ finally   ☐ first of all   ☐ then   ☐ meanwhile

b Show where you can add the following *which* clause to the paragraph:

which are small, flat pancakes popular in Russia

c Now add this *although* clause:

they can be eaten on their own or with jam

d Write the 'better' paragraph out in full in your notebook.

2 Complete this paragraph about sugar cane. Use the words and phrases in this list.

if   although   ~~which~~   which   in order to   when   until   as

Sugar cane is a tall grass, similar to bamboo, ^a ___which___ grows mainly in hot, wet countries. ^b _____ it needs a lot of water, it can grow in areas of low rainfall such as Egypt. There must, however, be plenty of irrigation water.

Small pieces of cane are planted in the fields and soon begin to grow. ^c _____ they are growing, the cane fields have to be weeded all the time. ^d _____ the cane is fully grown, it is cut a few centimetres above ground level. Sometimes the fields are burnt first ^e _____ burn off the leaves. ^f _____ the fields are not burnt, the leaves must be cut by hand. The cane is taken to the sugar factories. Here the cane is cut again into small lengths. It is then passed through a crushing machine, ^g _____ extracts all the juice. The juice is then boiled ^h _____ crystals of sugar are formed.

Free writing

3 Read the paragraph about making hummus on page 37 again. Now look at these notes for making 5-minute ice cream. Use the notes below to write a paragraph in your notebook explaining the process. Use passive verbs where possible. Add sequence words.

5-minute ice cream

You will need:

one bag of frozen berries (e.g., raspberries)

half a cup of sugar

two-thirds of a cup of heavy cream

a splash of pure vanilla extract

a food mixer

serving dishes

1 Place the frozen berries in a food mixer.

2 Pour in the cream and sugar.

3 Add a splash of vanilla.

4 Switch on the mixer.

5 Leave for about 30 seconds (until it becomes firm).

6 Pour the ice cream into serving bowls.

7 Place the bowls in the freezer if a more firm ice cream is required.

8 Remove bowls.

9 Add fruit for decoration if required.

10 Serve.

Note: You can also make it with yoghurt instead of cream.

4 Read the paragraph 'How to build a road' on page 39. Use the pictures to help you write a paragraph in your notebook about the process of building a skyscraper. Use passive verbs and sequence words.

5 Think of a dish or drink that you like. Write a paragraph in your notebook to describe how it is prepared.

Use this checklist to edit your writing in Exercises 3–5.

CHECKLIST	EXERCISE		
	3	4	5
How many sentences are there?			
How many full stops (.) are there?			
Does every sentence begin with a capital letter?			
Does every sentence have a verb?			
Have you checked your spelling?			
Can you make your writing better?			

Editing

 6 Check the verbs in this paragraph about cotton production. There are eight mistakes.

COTTON PRODUCTION

Cotton is grow in hot countries such as Egypt and parts of China. It needs plenty of water, either from rainfall or from irrigation, and good, rich soils. When the cotton will be ready, it must harvested quickly before rain can damage it. The cotton are sometimes picked by hand, but usually it is picked by machines. The cotton is collect and placed in machines, where the fibres (called 'lint') are separating from the cotton seeds. The lint is then packed into bales and send to factories where cotton cloth are manufactured.

 7 Look at this advertisement for the Paradise Restaurant. There are ten mistakes in spelling, punctuation and capital letters. Underline the mistakes and correct them.

Paradise Restaurant

Do you like delicious, spicy food servd in beautiful surroundings? Yes? Then visit our new 'paradise Restaurant'. We are locatd in Ocean Avenue in the centre of the city Our restaurant which has wonderful views of the city, is on the tetnh floor of the Toyota Tower. The menu, wich is prepared by our experienced chef contains Chinese, malaysian and Indonesian dishes. Although our prices are low you will find that the quality of the food is very haigh.

Come and visit us soon!

Vocabulary building

Describing construction

8 **Look at the table. Match the verbs on the left with the nouns across the top.**

Put a ✓ in the correct boxes and a ✗ in the incorrect ones. For example, you can build a bridge, but you cannot build an omelette. Some of the verbs match more than one noun.

	a bridge	a well	the foundations	a plan	a hole	an omelette
build	✓					✗
draw up						
lay						
construct						
make						
drill						
dig						

Describing recipes

9 **Match these verbs with the diagrams below.**

drain mix boil heat add pour steam measure cover

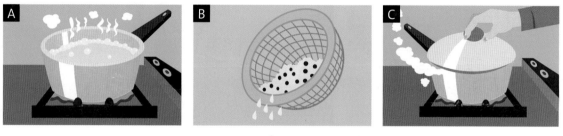

drain

Describing processes

 We use the verbs below when we describe how things are processed.
Match the verbs with the pictures.

| transport | cut | plant | collect | pick | pass through | pour into | spread | export |

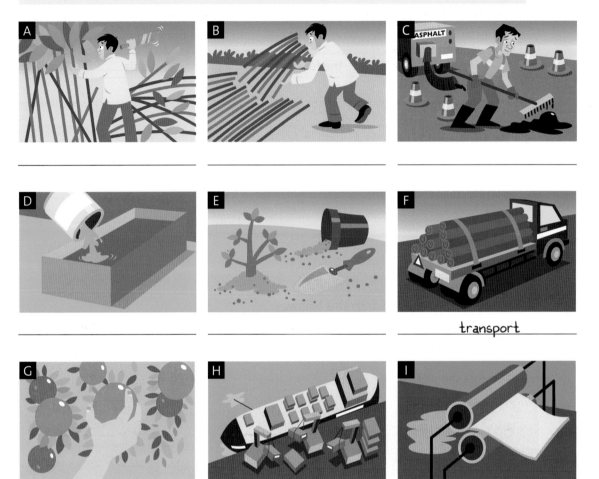

transport

Unit 3 Language review

A Past participles

A passive verb consists of two parts – the verb *to be* and a past participle:

To be	Past participle
is	made
are	put
can be	soaked
must be	drained

Past participles can be regular like **soaked** and **drained**.
They can also be irregular like **made** and **put**.

1 **Put the correct past participle into each of these sentences. They are all irregular.**

  a Sugar cane can be _____ by machine or by hand. (cut)

  b Most electrical goods are _____ in South East Asia. (make)

  c First, the drains have to be _____ . (dig)

  d When the ground is flat, the foundations are _____ . (lay)

  e Skyscrapers are usually _____ in the centre of cities, where land is expensive. (build)

  f Signals are _____ by mobile phones to special aerials. (send)

  g Photographs must be _____ of the site of the new town. (take)

  h Plans are usually _____ up by architects, engineers and planners. (draw)

  i Some planets can be _____ in the night sky without a telescope. (see)

  j Natural rubber trees are _____ in many parts of the world. (find)

2 **Read the paragraph below about new towns. Put the verb in brackets into the correct passive form.**

NEW TOWNS

The population of many areas of the world is growing rapidly. As a result there is a great need for new towns. One example is Shatin in the Hong Kong region of China. New towns such as Shatin **a** _____ usually _____ (build) in rural areas. Before construction can begin, the land **b** _____ (map) by surveyors. Aerial and satellite photos **c** _____ also _____ (need). The architects, planners and engineers look at the maps and plans **d** _____ (draw up) for the new town. When everyone has agreed on the plans, work can begin. First of all, roads **e** _____ (lay). Electric power and water **f** _____ (bring) to the site and drains **g** _____ (dig). Then buildings such as houses, apartment blocks, schools and shops **h** _____ (construct). Finally, trees and gardens **i** _____ (plant) in order to make the town more attractive.

B *By after passive verbs: By + noun, By + ...~ing*

The route is marked out	by surveyors.
TV channels can be changed	by using the remote control.

3 **Match these parts to make sentences. Write them in your notebook.**

a Meals are prepared	surgeons.
b Operations are carried out	announcers.
c Cars are repaired	everyone.
d The TV news is read	by mechanics.
e Houses are designed	cooks.
f Mobile phones are used	architects.

4 **Complete these sentences with *by + ...~ing*.**

a Ice cream can be made quickly _____

b Chickpeas are softened _____

c Food can be cooked in the desert _____

d The cursor is moved _____

e Sugar cane is collected _____

C *Also*

Hummus is popular in the Arab World. It is **also** popular in Greece and Turkey.
Perfume is produced in factories. It can **also** be made at home.
Maria studies IT at university. She **also** studies Business Administration.
Also comes **after** the verb *to be* and **modals**. It comes **before** the main verb.

5 **Add *also* to these sentences.**

a YouTube is very popular with young people. It is used by many older people.

_____

b Toni is a shop assistant during the day. He works in a restaurant in the evenings.

_____

c A paper copy of the essay can be submitted to the teacher. It may be sent by email.

_____

d Leopards are found in parts of Africa. They are found in the mountains of Oman.

_____

e Travel agents arrange flights and tickets for travellers. They can book hotels if required.

_____

f Supermarkets sell food and products for the house. Some supermarkets sell clothes.

_____

D *Which* clauses

What	*Which* clause	Verb + ...
The *road*,	**which** is named after a poem,	cuts through high mountains.
What?	**Verb + ...**	**Which clause**
The road	cuts through *mountains*,	**which** are over 1,500m in places.

6 Add these *which* clauses to the paragraph about rubber production. Write the letters a–e in the correct places.

Rubber is an important material for many products. It comes from rubber trees _____ but it can also be made synthetically. Natural rubber _____ is made from latex. The liquid latex is collected by cutting the bark of the tree. The latex runs slowly into a cup _____ . After a few hours the latex stops running. All of the cups are emptied and the latex is collected in a tanker _____ . The tanker takes the latex to the factory and the process begins. First, acid is added in order to solidify the rubber. The rubber forms thick strips. They are turned into flat sheets _____ . Finally, the sheets are then packed and exported to countries all over the world.

a which is usually located nearby

b which are made thinner by passing through rollers

c which is attached to the tree

d which is a white liquid produced by rubber trees

e which grow in hot, humid regions

Now write out the paragraph in your notebook. Remember to use the correct punctuation.

7 Add *which* clauses to the sentences below.

a My friend lives in Ankara, _____ .

b Tablets, _____ , have become very popular in recent years.

c Hurricanes, _____ , often affect the islands of the Caribbean in the summer months.

d One of most popular fast foods is pizza, _____ .

e I am studying accounting at the MT College, _____ .

E *Although* clauses

Although Gunter is a professor of Physics, he doesn't know how to boil and egg.

Gunter doesn't know how to boil an egg, **although he is a professor of Physics**.

8 Put these words and phrases in the correct order. Write them on the lines below. They all contain *although* clauses. Add the correct punctuation.

a and decided / it was only nine o'clock / Tariq felt tired / to go to bed / although

_____

_____

b a successful businesswoman / didn't go / Maria / to university / she became / although

_____

_____

c very expensive at the moment / many Indians love / although / to buy gold / it is

_____

_____

d to make it at home / hummus is available / prefer / in supermarkets / many people / although

_____

_____

e she can't speak it / Sue / for three years / studied Cantonese / very well / although

_____

_____

9 Add *although* clauses to these sentences.

a I love to eat ice cream, _____

b My computer has broken down, _____

c I managed to complete the essay in the library _____

d _____ I arrived on time for the exam.

e _____ we enjoyed the picnic.

A Focus on the sentence

Looking at text

1 Read Victor's story. He is explaining what happened to him on a boat trip. Choose a picture – A, B or C – to go with the story.

Victor's story

I had a terrible experience a few days ago. I went fishing with a friend of mine, Carlos, who has a small fishing boat. We left the harbour just after lunch. Although it <u>had rained</u> in the morning, it was a fine, sunny afternoon. The boat was quite fast and after travelling for about an hour, we could no longer see land. We <u>were heading</u> for an old wreck, which was a favourite fishing spot. Suddenly the engine <u>stopped</u>. There was silence. 'What's the problem?' I asked Carlos. 'We've run out of petrol,' he replied. 'But don't worry,' he said. 'We've got some petrol in this can.' He bent down to lift a metal container from the bottom of the boat. As he opened the container his expression changed. 'Oh,' he said. 'It's empty!' Carlos explained that his nephew had used the boat yesterday. 'He probably forgot to fill up the spare can,' he said. I looked around us, but there were no boats in sight and no sight of land. I was beginning to feel worried. There were some dark clouds to the south and the wind was getting stronger. In the distance I could hear thunder.

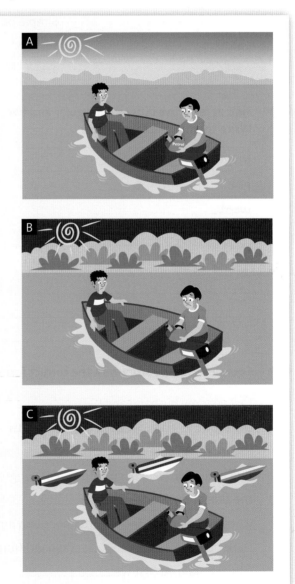

LANGUAGE: simple past tense

When we tell a story we mainly use verbs in the simple past tense.

I **had** a terrible experience a few days ago.
I **went** fishing with a friend of mine, Carlos.
Suddenly, the engine **stopped**.
'What's the problem?', I **asked** Carlos.

Irregular verbs

Verb	Simple past	Past participle
have	had	had
go	went	gone

Regular verbs (infinitive + *ed*)

Verb	Simple past	Past participle
stop	stopped	stopped
ask	asked	asked

2 **Find at least five different irregular and five regular simple past verbs in the text on page 55. Write them in the table below.**

Irregular verbs	Regular verbs
had	stopped
went	asked

3 **Complete Sarah's story with the correct form of these verbs. Use simple past verbs.**

Last year my husband and I _____ (decide) to visit my aunt, who lives in the east of the country. I hadn't seen her for at least two years. We _____ (leave) very early in the morning, because my aunt's home is about 600km from where we live. After driving for about two hours, we were beginning to feel hungry. We _____ (find) a small restaurant by the side of the road and _____ (have) a good breakfast. Then we _____ (continue) our journey, but after about an hour the weather _____ (begin) to change. Dark clouds _____ (appear) from the west and suddenly it _____ (start) to rain. At first we _____ (be) able to continue driving but soon the rain _____ (become) very heavy and there _____ (be) thunder and lightning.

LANGUAGE: past continuous tense

We can also use the past continuous tense when we tell a story. This tense describes an action that continued over a period of time in the past.

We **were heading** for an old shipwreck.
I **was having** a great time.

Or an action that ends suddenly.

I **was sleeping** when suddenly my phone rang.

to be (was/were)	+ ~ing
were	heading
was	having
was	sleeping

 4 Find three examples of past continuous verbs in Victor and Sarah's stories on page 55 and 56. Write them in the table below.

to be (was/were)	+ ~ing
were	heading

LANGUAGE: past perfect

**We use the past perfect to describe something that began before the story began.
We can call it 'the past in the past'.**

Although it had rained in the morning, it was a fine sunny afternoon.

Past in the past	Story	Now
It had rained in the morning.	It was a fine afternoon.	

The past perfect consists of **had** + past participle.
It **had rained** in the morning.

5 Find two more examples of the past perfect tense from Victor and Sarah's stories and add them to the table.

had	+ past participle
had	rained

6   **Read Christina's story. Find out where Christina and Sonia live.**

An interesting thing happened to me last year. I flew to Miami with my family for three weeks. We were staying in an apartment not far from downtown Miami. One evening we went for a walk to the harbour, Bayside, which was not far from the apartment. My uncle, who knows Miami very well, wanted to take us to have some Cuban food. Suddenly I saw an old friend, Sonia. It was a wonderful surprise, I hadn't seen her since I left school in Salvador six years ago. I had heard that she had got married and had gone to live in Belo Horizonte. After greeting each other, I asked her if she was still living in Belo Horizonte. 'No', she said, 'my husband got a job in Rio de Janeiro. We have been there for two years.' I told her that I also lived in Rio. 'We bought an apartment there last month,' I said. Sonia asked me which part of Rio I lived in. I explained that the apartment was in the suburbs, opposite a football stadium. 'Is it a very large building with blue balconies?' asked Sonia. I told her that it was. I was rather surprised, and asked her how she knew the building so well. 'We live in the same building!' she explained.

a   Where did Christina go last year?

She went to Miami.

b   Where were they staying?

_____

c   Why was Christina surprised when she met Sonia?

_____

d   Why did Sonia move from Belo Horizonte to Rio?

_____

e   Why did Sonia know Christina's building so well?

_____

LANGUAGE: reporting speech

When we tell a story we often report what people said. We use reporting verbs for this.

say, tell, ask, reply, explain.

We can report **directly**:
'What's the problem?' I asked Carlos.
'We've run out of petrol,' he replied.

Or we can report **indirectly**:
Carlos explained that his nephew had used the boat yesterday.
I told her that I also lived in Rio.

7   **Read Victor's story again. Put a circle around the reporting verbs. Add them to the list.**

asked   replied

_____

Read Christina's story. Circle the reporting verbs and add them to the list.

asked   said

_____

LANGUAGE: *say* and *tell*

We use *say* (*said*) in indirect and direct speech.

Carlos **said**: 'There is no petrol.'
Carlos **said** there was no petrol.

We use *tell* (*told*) in indirect speech. *Tell* must be followed by an object (*me, the man, everyone,* etc.)

Carlos **told** me there was no petrol. ✓
Carlos told there was no petrol. ✗

8 **Add these reporting verbs to the sentences below:**

said   ~~told~~   explained   replied   asked

a I <u>told</u>_____ Sonia that I also lived in Rio.

b I _____ that my husband had been offered a new job at the university and we had decided to move there a few months ago.

c 'How do you like Rio?' _____ Sonia. 'It's great,' I _____ .

d Sonia _____ that she liked it too. They hoped to stay there for many years.

9 **Read this newspaper report. What are the people in the pictures saying? Use direct speech.**

12 NEWS

Mumbai Plane Crash

AN aeroplane that was trying to land at Mumbai airport crashed into the sea yesterday. Fortunately all the passengers were rescued. Many had cuts and bruises and some had to go to hospital. The plane was flying from Amman to Mumbai.

Ahmed Said, who was going to visit relatives in India, said that he was reading when he heard a loud bang. 'I looked out of the window,' Ahmed explained, 'and saw smoke. I told the stewardess that one of the engines was on fire. Then the pilot spoke to the passengers over the intercom system. He told us that we were going to land in the sea.

The stewardess told us to put on our life jackets,' said Ahmed, 'and after that I began to pray.' Ahmed explained what had happened after landing on the water. 'Everything was very quiet for a few seconds,' he said, 'and then everyone got up and went towards the emergency exits, which were now open. From there we could see the water a few metres below. Fortunately it was calm and we got into the rescue boats safely.'

A spokeswoman for International Air said that it was their first accident. 'We don't know what caused the engine to explode. It's a mystery,' she said. ■

Read these sentences from the newspaper article. What (or who) do the underlined words refer to?

a Fortunately all the passengers were rescued. <u>Many</u> had cuts and bruises and <u>some</u> had to go to hospital.

The passengers _____

b Then the pilot spoke to the passengers ... <u>He</u> told <u>us</u> that we were going to land in the sea.

_____

c Everyone got up and went towards the emergency exits, which were now open. From <u>there</u> we could see the water a few metres below.

_____

d A spokeswoman for International Air said that it was <u>their</u> first accident.

_____

Sentence building

LANGUAGE: direct and indirect speech

Look at these examples:

a Carlos said, 'I feel cold.'
b Carlos said (**that**) he felt cold.

Example a is **direct** speech.
Example b is **indirect** speech.

What are the four things that are different in b?

 Complete the rules about tenses.

In indirect (or reported) speech:

a the simple present becomes the past _____ tense.

b the simple past becomes the _____ tense.

c the present perfect becomes the _____ tense.

d the present continuous becomes the _____ tense.

e modals (*can*, *will*, etc.) change to _____ , etc.

 Underline the verbs in the direct and indirect speech in these sentences.

Direct	Indirect
Sonia said, 'I live in Rio.'	Sonia said that she lived in Rio.
Carlos said, 'My nephew borrowed the boat'.	Carlos said that his nephew had borrowed the boat.
'I've never run out of petrol before,' Carlos said.	Carlos said that he had never run out of petrol before.
'It's starting to rain,' said Sarah.	Sarah said that it was starting to rain.
I said, 'I can't swim.'	I said that I couldn't swim.
'I will phone you tomorrow,' Christina said.	Christina said she would phone me tomorrow.

13 These sentences all contain indirect speech. Put the words in the correct order and write them in the table below.

a that / said / cancelled / teacher / the / was / the / class

b late / she / Miriam / us / be / told / that / would

c that / with / there / engine / was / said / the / the / a problem / pilot

d policeman / drive / carefully / told / more / me / the / to

e said / had / week / Faisal / his cousin / the car / that / used / last

Who	*said/told* (me)	*(that)*	Indirect speech	.
Sonia	said	that	she had moved there last year	.
a				
b				
c				
d				
e				

14 Report these statements using *said* or *told me/us*.

a Zainab said

b Our teacher told us

c The man

d Abdullah

e The woman

f The young man

Joining ideas

LANGUAGE: *after/before ...~ing*

Look at these sentences:

The plane lost an engine.	The plane crashed into the sea.

We can join these sentences with *after*:

After the plane lost an engine, it crashed into the sea.	OR	After losing an engine, the plane crashed into the sea.

Mei Lin read the instructions.	Mei Lin switched on the machine.

We can also join sentences with *before*:

Before Mei Lin switched on the machine, she read the instructions.	OR	Before switching on the machine, Mei Lin read the instructions.

 Join these sentences using *after/before ...~ing*. Write the new sentences in your notebook. Remember to use commas.

a   John had a large lunch. John fell asleep for twenty minutes. (after)

   After a large lunch, John fell asleep for twenty minutes.

b   Make sure you check that there is enough petrol. Start the boat. (before)

c   We lived in Rome for six years. We moved to Istanbul. (after)

d   Nina tried on the dress. Nina bought the dress. (before)

e   Mike wrote the letter. Mike faxed the letter to the head office in Cairo. (after)

f   Ibn Battuta visited Mecca. Ibn Battuta travelled to China. (before)

LANGUAGE: *who* **clauses**

***Who* clauses tell us something extra about a person (or people). They can come in the middle of a sentence:**

Dr Martinez has been a lecturer in the college for many years.
Dr Martinez is the new head of the department.

Who?	*Who* clause	Last part of the sentence
Dr Martinez,	who is the new head of the department,	has been a lecturer in the college for many years.

***Who* clauses can also come at the end of a sentence.**

I went shopping with my cousin.
My cousin is staying with me for a few weeks.

First part of the sentence	Who?	*Who* clause
I went shopping with	my cousin,	who is staying with me for a few weeks.

16 **Join these sentences using *who* clauses. Remember to use commas. Write the new sentences in your notebook.**

a Ronaldo scored six goals last week. Ronaldo is an excellent football player.

Ronaldo, who is an excellent football player, scored six goals last week.

b I've just had a phone call from my sister. My sister is studying at a college in Manila.

c The mechanic said he could repair the car by the following day. The mechanic was very experienced.

d This morning I went to see the doctor. The doctor said I should rest for three days.

e Mohsin is reading a book about Atatürk. Atatürk was the founder of modern Turkey.

f Our English teacher is probably the best teacher in the college. Our English teacher is very kind, hard-working and helpful.

 17 **Add your own *who* clauses to these sentences. They are all about famous people. Write the new sentences in your notebook.**

a Ibn Battuta travelled to many countries, including Spain, Russia and China.

Ibn Battuta, who is considered to be one of the greatest travellers of all time, travelled to many countries including Spain, Russia and China.

b One of the most famous people in the world is the South Korean singer Park Jae-sang.

c Gandhi died in India in 1948.

d One of the richest men in the world is Bill Gates.

e Mrs Thatcher was Prime Minister of the United Kingdom from 1979 to 1990.

f Omar Khayam is most famous as the author of the *Rubaiyat*.

Now write three sentences in your notebook about people you know. Use *who* clauses.

Punctuation

 18 **These sentences all contain *who* clauses. Add commas, full stops and capital letters if they are needed.**

a the pathans who come from the mountainous regions of pakistan speak pashto as their mother tongue

b anna who has just graduated from the university of singapore wants to be an economist

c the druze are a religious sect who live mainly in the mountainous regions of Lebanon and southern syria

d my uncle who doesn't speak a word of english told me that he is planning to visit america in the summer

e yesterday I went to visit my grandmother who is in hospital with a chest complaint

f italians who are well-known for their love of music have some of the world's greatest opera singers

19 **Punctuate these sentences containing *after* and *before*.**

a after walking for six miles in the hot sun the man finally found a garage

b before cooking the sardines they washed them and cut them into pieces

c after landing in the sea and waiting for the rescue boats the passengers finally escaped

d before going on a boat trip make sure that there is petrol in the spare can

20 **Study the direct speech in the earlier paragraphs and in the example below.**

'What's happened?' I asked Carlos.
'We've run out of petrol,' he replied.

Now punctuate these sentences.

a id like a single room he told the receptionist

b whats the time carlos asked six oclock I replied

c follow the london road and turn left at the roundabout explained tania

d its very hot today said boris I think ill go for a swim

B Focus on the paragraph

Better paragraphs

1 **Read this paragraph from Nina's blog about a children's birthday party.**
What happened to the cake and orange juice?

On Saturday, Gabriella (1) invited me to her house. She was having a small party for her daughter, Elena. My father (2) offered to take me in his car and I arrived about two o'clock. The house (3) was full of people. There was a lot of noise from the children (4). Gabriella asked me if I wanted to meet Elena's teacher. I said 'Yes,' and so she took me into the garden and I was introduced to Koula (5). Gabriella brought us both some orange juice and a huge chocolate cake (6). I want to be a teacher too and so I asked Koula many questions about teaching. She told me that she had studied at a teacher training college in Thessaloniki (7). After leaving college, she went to teach in a small village school. Three years ago she moved to Athens and started teaching at Elena's school (8). I asked her what she liked most about teaching. 'The children,' she replied. 'They are lovely.' At that moment, the ball landed on the table and knocked the cake and orange juice onto the ground. 'Well, I like them most of the time,' she added with a smile.

Now add this 'extra information' to the paragraph. Match the clauses with the numbers (1–8) in the text. Then write out the paragraph in full in your notebook.

a who was sitting under a tree ☐

b who doesn't work on Saturdays ☐

c which is only half a kilometre from her home ☐

d who were playing with a plastic beach ball ☐

e who is a very close friend of mine ☐

f which she had baked for Elena's party ☐

g which is a large city in the north east of Greece ☐

h which was quite large ☐

2 **Read this story about three sailors and a genie. Complete each paragraph with the missing verbs.**

| ate | saw | were becoming | ~~were shipwrecked~~ | picked | up | was | jumped out |

A Many years ago three sailors ^a were shipwrecked on a small desert island in the middle of the ocean. They ^b_____ only raw fish and coconuts and after many months they ^c_____ very thin and weak. One day they ^d_____ a bottle floating in the water. One of the sailors ^e_____ it ^f_____ and took out the cork. There ^g_____ a flash of light and a genie suddenly ^h_____ of the bottle.

| asked | could ask | had rescued | replied | ~~spoke~~ | said | explained |

B The genie bowed and ⁱ spoke _____ to them. 'I am the genie of the bottle,' he ^j_____ politely. 'Your wish is my command.' He ^k_____ that because they ^l_____ him from the bottle they ^m_____ for three wishes. 'Anything we want?' ⁿ_____ the first sailor. 'Yes, anything,' ^o_____ the genie. But remember: only three wishes – one each!'

| disappeared | asked | was | bring | ~~explained~~ | told | clapped |

C The first sailor then ^p explained _____ that he missed his family very much and ^q_____ the genie to send him home. The genie clapped his hands. Suddenly there ^r_____ a flash and the first sailor disappeared. 'That was marvellous!' said the second sailor. He then ^s_____ the genie that he missed his shipmates. He would like to go back to his old ship and join them. Again the genie ^t_____ his hands and the second sailor ^u_____. The third sailor, who was now alone, suddenly felt very sad. 'What would you like?' the genie asked him. 'I feel lonely', said the third sailor. 'Please ^v_____ my two friends back to the island!'

3 **Answer these questions about the story in your own words.**

a Why were the sailors on the island?
The sailors were on the island because they had been shipwrecked.

b Why were they becoming thin?
_____

c What happened when they saw the bottle?
_____

d What did the genie offer the three sailors?
_____

e What did the first sailor want?
_____

f What did the second sailor want?
_____

g How did the third sailor feel?
_____

h What did he want?
_____

4 **Use these words to complete the paragraph.**

before   which   in order to   if   when   that   although   after   who   ~~who~~

The famous 5,000-metre runner Naseem Ahmed arrived in Tunis today. Naseem, ᵃ who
was born in Yemen but now lives in Germany, was met at the airport by many fans and journalists.
He told the crowd ᵇ_____ he was very happy to be in Tunisia, ᶜ_____ he was sorry
that it was only a short visit. Naseem has come to Tunisia ᵈ_____ take part in the African
Championship, ᵉ_____ starts tomorrow. ᶠ_____ visiting Tunis, Naseem will travel to
Morocco, ᵍ_____ returning to Germany at the end of the month. One journalist asked him
ʰ_____ he thought he would win the race. 'I'm not sure,' he replied, 'there are a lot of good
runners in the race. It'll be hard.' Naseem, ⁱ_____ is well known for his modesty and good
sportsmanship, became famous ʲ_____ he won an Olympic gold medal for the
5,000 metres two years ago.

Free writing

5 **Read Victor's story again on page 55. How do you think the story ends? Did they get back home again? How? Write a paragraph in your notebook. Remember to use the past simple, past continuous and past perfect tenses.**

6 **Read Sarah's story again on page 56. How does this story end? Did the couple complete the journey? What happened to them after the storm? Write a paragraph in your notebook. Remember to use the past simple, past continuous and past perfect tenses.**

7 **Read Christina's paragraph again on page 58. Now imagine you are Sonia. Write about the meeting with Christina in your notebook. Use some direct and indirect speech.**

8 **A TV reporter is interviewing Gita, one of the cabin crew on the Mumbai plane that crashed. Read the interview. Now imagine you are Gita. Write the story of the crash in your notebook. Begin like this:**

A few days ago I was flying from Amman in Jordan to Mumbai.

REPORTER: Do you work for International Air?

GITA: Yes, I do. I've been with them for five years.

REPORTER: Can you tell me what happened on the flight?

GITA: Well, I was serving coffee when I heard a loud bang. I looked out of the window and saw that one of the engines was on fire.

REPORTER: What did you do?

GITA: I went to the cockpit and reported the fire to the captain.

REPORTER: What happened next?

GITA: The captain spoke to the passengers. Then I explained how to put the lifejackets on. I tried to keep everyone calm. Then we hit the water and I helped everyone off the plane and into the boats.

REPORTER: Were you afraid?

GITA: Not really. I was too busy to think about crashing.

REPORTER: Will you fly again?

GITA: Yes. In fact, I'm scheduled to fly next week.

9 **Write about an interesting thing that happened to you. What happened? Where were you? Report what you said and what other people said. Use your notebook.**

Use this checklist to edit your writing in Exercises 5–9.

CHECKLIST	EXERCISE				
	5	6	7	8	9
How many sentences are there?					
How many full stops (.) are there?					
Does every sentence begin with a capital letter?					
Does every sentence have a verb?					
Have you checked your spelling?					
Can you make your writing better?					

Editing

10 Read the beginning of this story. There are five spelling mistakes, five mistakes in punctuation and five grammatical mistakes. Find the mistakes and correct them. Then write the paragraph out in full in your notebook.

One day last summer my family went for a picnac in a park near the sea. We leave home early in the morning and found a quiet place under some trees We put up the tent, which we always take with us and my sister and I began to prepare some food. After eating, we was all resting near the tint and Somboon, which is my youngest son, was playing with a ball. I told him to go and blay near the trees. A few minutes later he screamed and fell to the ground. We all ran over and found him holding his foet. What's the matter?' I ask. 'Its my foot,' he cried. 'Something bit me.' Then we see a large scorpion in the grass.

I told my husband to kill it quickly. He picked up a stick and hit it hard until it was no longer moving. Then he said he would take somboon to the hospital. We all went with him in the jeep. I was very waried because Somboon was breathing with difficulty.

Vocabulary building

Reporting verbs

11 Find the reporting verbs. They are all in the past tense.

a i d a s _said_____ **b** d e l i n x a e p_____

c d o l t_____ **d** s e d k a_____

e d e d a d_____ **f** l i d e r p e_____

Describing emotions

12 Make two lists from these adjectives. One for words similar to *worried*, and one for words similar to *calm*.

~~nervous~~ ~~relaxed~~ afraid tranquil frightened concerned
peaceful anxious quiet tense still

worried _nervous_____ _____ _____

_____ _____ _____

calm _relaxed_____ _____ _____

_____ _____ _____

Use these clues to complete the crossword below. Most of the words are in this unit.

Across

1 The line where the sky meets the sea. (7 letters)

4 'Would you like ___ or coffee?' the waiter asked. (3)

6 The boys said that they had ___ their homework and so I let them watch TV. (4)

7 Carlos and Victor got into trouble because the spare can was ___ . (5)

12 Park Jae-sang, ___ is famous for his music videos, comes from the Gangnam district of Seoul. (3)

13 My son ___ when the snake bit him. (8)

14 ___ we were walking along Edgware Road, I met an old friend. (2)

16 To hit the hands together. (4)

17 There were ___ clouds in the distance. I thought it would rain. (4)

19 The stewardess told us to ___ on our lifejackets. (3)

21 'How do you ___ ?' the doctor asked. 'Terrible,' I replied. (4)

22 Boris told me that he ___ swim very well. (5)

24 Last ___ I visited Turkey. (4)

25 We usually use the past simple tense ___ we tell a story. (4)

Down

1 Peter explained that he ___ left the keys to the car in a different jacket. (3)

2 Usain Bolt and Haile Gebrselassie are famous ___. (7)

3 Several passengers were injured and ___ man had to go to hospital. (3)

4 'I'm going to ___ to land the plane in the sea,' said the pilot. (3)

5 ___ it was a sunny day, the wind was very cold. (8)

8 Prime Minister or afternoon. (2)

9 Hassan said ___ he was going to be late for the meeting. (4)

10 Suzanna ___ me if I wanted to go for a walk. (5)

11 I ___ that I was feeling rather tired. (7)

12 I ___ heading for the shop when I saw my friend Anne. (3)

14 In order to ___ for a place at the university, it is necessary to fill in a form. (5)

15 All right! (2)

18 ___, which is grown in Egypt, needs plenty of water and high temperatures. (4) [from Unit 3]

20 Travelling by plane is safer ___ travelling by car. (4)

21 Salem told me that he was going to ___ to Jakarta next week. (3)

23 Ahmed told the stewardess that the engine was ___ fire. (2)

Unit 4 Language review

A Past tenses

When we tell a story we mainly use verbs in the simple past tense.

I **had** a terrible experience a few days ago.
Suddenly, the engine **stopped**.

Irregular verb	Simple past	Past participle
have	had	had

Regular verb	Simple past (+ ~ed)	Past participle
stop	stopped	stopped

 1 Complete this story of the film *The Life of Pi* with verbs in the simple past tense.

The film, *The Life of Pi*, is very popular, although it is a rather strange story. It is about a boy and a tiger in a boat. The boy is Indian. Many years ago his father

a_____ (own) a zoo in India. As a boy, Pi, **b**_____ (grow) up in the zoo, so he

c_____ (know) all the animals.

Unfortunately the zoo was losing money. One day his father **d**_____ (decide) to move to America with his family and all of the animals from the zoo. Pi and the rest of the family **e**_____ (be) not happy about this but they **f**_____ (have) to do what their father wanted. The animals were **g**_____ (put) on a ship in cages. After a few days, while they were sailing in the Pacific Ocean, there **h**_____ (be) a terrible storm. The ship **i**_____ (sink) and most of the passengers and the animals **j**_____ (die). Only Pi and a tiger **k**_____ (survive). Because he was a good swimmer Pi **l**_____ (can swim) from the sinking ship to a lifeboat. But when he **m**_____ (climb) into the lifeboat he **n**_____ (have) a big surprise. He **o**_____ (find) the tiger from the zoo in the back of the boat. For the rest of the journey across the ocean he **p**_____ (share) the boat with this dangerous animal.

We also use the past continuous tense when we tell a story. This tense describes an action that continued over a period of time in the past – or an action that ends suddenly.

We **were heading** for an old shipwreck.   I **was sleeping** when suddenly my phone rang.

to be (was/were)	+ ~ing
were	heading
was	sleeping

2 **Look at the sentences below. Put the verbs in brackets into the past continuous or simple past forms.**

a There _____ (be) a small earthquake at 10.30 last night.

I _____ (sleep) and my sisters _____ (watch) TV.

b The company's sales _____ (fall) steadily last year until the new manager

_____ (arrive) and sales improved dramatically.

c It _____ (rain) heavily last night and so I _____ (drive)

along the motorway very carefully. Suddenly a lorry _____ (brake) hard just

in front of me. I _____ (can stop) in time and _____

(crash) into it.

d The first geologists _____ (come) to Bahrain to search for underground

water. But while they _____ (look) for water they _____

(find) oil.

We use the past perfect to describe something that began before the story began – 'the past in the past'.

Although it **had rained** in the morning, it was a fine sunny afternoon.
We went to the cinema last week but I didn't enjoy it. I **had seen** the film before.

Past in the past	Story	Now
It had rained in the morning.	It was a fine afternoon.	

had	+ past participle
had	rained
had	seen

3 **Complete these sentences using the past perfect. The notes will help you.**

a The food was wonderful but I didn't eat much because _____ .
(eat/earlier)

b The farmers were very happy when it started to rain. It _____ .
(not rain/six months)

c When Ali went to France last year he couldn't speak the language although he _____

_____ . (study/six years/school)

d Everyone was pleased when Ferdinand got promotion last month.

He _____ . (work/very hard)

e I was surprised when I met Bino last week. I thought _____ .
(move/Australia)

B Direct and indirect speech

Look at the examples:

Direct	Indirect
a Sonia said, '**I live** in Rio'.	Sonia said **that she lived** in Rio.
b Carlos said, 'My nephew **borrowed** the boat'.	Carlos said that his nephew **had borrowed** the boat.
c '**It's starting** to rain,' said Sarah.	Sarah said that it **was starting** to rain.
d I said, 'I **can't** swim.'	I said that I **couldn't** swim.

 4 **Change these sentences into indirect speech. Make changes in punctuation.**

a Lee said, 'I'll give you the money later.'

_____

b Andy said, 'I am studying Engineering at MRT University.'

_____

c Hari said, 'I don't speak Malay, but I can read it.'

_____

d Dr Hussain said, 'The treatment has been successful.'

_____

e Stefani said, 'I work in a clothing factory, but I am looking for another job.'

_____

5 *Say* or *tell*? Write *said* or *told* in these sentences.

a Yuki _____ she would be here by now!

b The lecturer _____ the students that the exam had been cancelled.

c The manager _____ his assistant to write the report again.

d Salem _____ he was planning to visit Indonesia next year.

e The football coach _____ the players that they had to play better in the next game.

f Suzi _____ that her car had broken down on the motorway and she would be late.

C *After/Before*

Look:

The plane lost an engine.	The plane crashed into the sea.

After losing an engine, the plane crashed into the sea.
After the plane lost an engine, it crashed into the sea.

Mei Lin read the instructions.	Mei Lin switched on the machine.

Before switching on the machine, Mei Lin read the instructions.
Before Mei Lin switched on the machine, she read the instructions.

6   **Put these words in the correct order to form a sentence. They all contain *after* and *before* structures.**

a   the battery / the phone / fully charging / ready / to use / is / after

_____

b   is boiling / placing / in the pan / make sure / the eggs / before / the water

_____

c   to the address / you complete / send it / after / at the top of the page / the form

_____

d   dark glasses / put on / entered / they / before / the bank / the robbers

_____

e   a new mobile / Sonia / several websites / to compare / before / prices / checked / buying

_____

D *Who* clauses

Who clauses give us extra information about a person or people.
Look:

Who?	*Who* clause	Last part of sentence
Dr Martinez,	who is the new head of the department,	has been a lecturer in the college for many years.
Last part of sentence	**Who?**	***Who* clause**
I went shopping with	my cousin,	who is staying with me for a few weeks.

7   **Put these words in the correct order to make sentences. They all contain *who* clauses.**
Write them out with the correct punctuation.

a   all over the world / who / a pilot / flies / is / for British Airways / my brother

_____

b   watching / who / the world's fastest runner / during the Olympics / I enjoyed / Usain Bolt / is

_____

c   will teach us / our new professor / I met / yesterday / next semester / Physics / who

_____

d   lives / in Indonesia / last night / was chatting / with a close friend / I / who

_____

8   **Add *who* clauses to these sentence.**

a   After the accident Afzal saw a doctor, who _____

b   The founder of Apple Corporation was Steve Jobs, who _____

c   Christopher Columbus, who _____ , was born in Italy.

d   My brother is a diplomat and last year he met Ban Ki-moon, who _____

e   Lionel Messi, who _____ , plays for the Barcelona FC in the Spanish league.

Which is better?

A Focus on the sentence

Looking at text

1 Kate is writing to Aunt Sarah's problem page in a magazine. Kate has two options. What are they?

EDINBURGH

EXETER

> Dear Aunt Sarah,
>
> I have to make a difficult decision. Next year I want to go to college in order to continue my studies. I'd like to do a teacher training course. However, the college which has the most suitable course is in Exeter, nearly 500 miles from Edinburgh. I like Exeter. It's a lovely city, and it has a good climate. In fact the climate is <u>better than</u> Edinburgh's. It's warmer in the winter and it's <u>less windy</u>. But it's smaller than Edinburgh and I think I would find life less interesting there. It's also a very long way from my family and friends, who all live close to Edinburgh. I think I would be lonely! It would also be more expensive for me to live in Exeter. I would have to pay for student accommodation, whereas in Edinburgh I can live with my family. There's a college which I could go to in Edinburgh. However, it doesn't have the course that I really want to do. What should I do, Aunt Sarah? I don't know you, but you are the best person to ask!
>
> *Kate*

2 Read the letter again and complete the notes in the table below.
It shows the points for and against Exeter.

For	Against
lovely city	smaller than Edinburgh

3 **Read Aunt Sarah's reply. Where does she think Kate should study?**

Dear Kate,

It's always difficult to make a decision like this. On the one hand, you don't want to leave your family and friends in Edinburgh, but on the other hand, you want to be a teacher and the most suitable course is in Exeter. Personally, I think you should go to study in Exeter, even though living in Edinburgh would be less expensive. It sounds like a lovely place to me. I agree, too, that the winters there are more comfortable than in Edinburgh, which sometimes seems the coldest place in the world when the east wind is blowing!

However, the climate is not the most important thing. You must take the course which is best for you. In this case, we know that the most suitable course is in Exeter. Although you'll miss your family at first, I think you'll soon make friends in Exeter. Is there a flight from Exeter to Edinburgh? That would be the quickest way to get home. Then you could visit Edinburgh sometimes at the weekend. Remember, this is an important decision – perhaps one of the most important decisions that you will make. Try to find a friend or a member of the family who you can talk to.

Aunt Sarah

a What must Kate do when choosing a course?

_____

b What does Aunt Sarah tell Kate to do at weekends?

_____

c What else does she advise Kate to do?

_____

LANGUAGE: comparatives

Look at these sentences:

Exeter is **smaller than** Edinburgh.
Exeter's climate is **better than** Edinburgh's climate.
The course in Exeter is **more interesting than** the course in Edinburgh.
Living in Edinburgh would be **less expensive than** living in Exeter.

There are two comparative forms.

1 With **short** adjectives, like *small, big, fast, cheap* and *heavy*, we add ~*er* to the adjective:

smaller, bigger, faster, cheaper, heavier

2 With most **long** adjectives (two syllables or more), like *interesting, pleasant* and *comfortable*, we add ***more*** before the adjective:

Handwritten letters are **more** interesting than email.

Note:

a Some short adjectives (e.g., *good, bad*) are irregular. They change their form to make the comparative (e.g., *better than, worse than*).

b The opposite of *more* is ***less***: Email is **less** interesting than handwritten letters.

4 **Put the adjective in brackets into the correct form. Check the spelling of the comparative form.**

a New York is colder_____ (cold) than Miami in winter.

b I think books are _____ (interesting) than computer games.

c A laptop is _____ (heavy) than a tablet.

d Which is _____ (useful) to study – History or Geography?

e China is a _____ (large) country than Australia.

f Trains are usually _____ (fast) than buses.

g Old buildings are _____ (beautiful) than many modern buildings.

LANGUAGE: superlatives

Look at these sentences:

Bangkok has **the tallest** hotel in South East Asia. It is 319m, and has 89 storeys.
The best time to visit Korea is in the spring.
The White House is **the most famous** building in Washington.
The Life of Pi is the **most interesting** film I have seen this year.

We use the superlative forms ~est and *the most* if we are comparing more than two things.
The opposite of **the most** is **the least**.

At my old school **the least popular** subject was History.

---

5 **Read through Kate's letter and Aunt Sarah's reply again. Underline examples of comparative and superlative forms. The first two examples have already been underlined. Add two examples to each box.**

Comparative *~er than*	Comparative *more/less ... than*
better than	less windy

Superlatives *the ~est*	Superlatives *the most/the least ...*
the best	the most suitable

6 **Put these adjectives into the superlative form. Use *the ~est* or *the most* ...**

a The Burj Khalifa was the tallest_____ (tall) building in the world in 2014.

b Last year Google was _____ (popular) website on the Internet.

c Michael Jackson is still one of _____ (famous) people in the world.

d The Utama Shopping Centre is _____ (big) shopping mall in Malaysia.

e Mercury is _____ (close) planet to the sun, followed by Venus and the Earth.

f Bollywood is _____ (productive) film industry in the world.

It produces even more films than Hollywood.

7 **Sam and Yoko are writing about books and eReaders. Answer these questions:**

a Which does Sam prefer? b Which does Yoko prefer?

Sam

I have a new eReader. It's very convenient when I travel because it fits into a jacket pocket. I can download books easily and read what I want, and when I want. I already have six books, which I downloaded from Amazon, stored on the reader. The eReader is also much lighter than a book. Imagine if I had to carry six books! However, to be honest, I still prefer a 'paper' book. Reading a book is a more enjoyable experience. I like the smell and the feel of a new book. I like looking at the cover. I can also go backwards and forwards easily to reread something, whereas it seems more difficult to find your way around an eBook. Most of all I like to see the books on my shelf. People who are interested can look at them easily and borrow them if they want. Of course you can let people see your eReader, but it is not the same as having books on your bookshelves. I agree that books are less convenient for travelling. I will probably just use my eReader for long trips.

Yoko

I used to love paper books and I had many on my shelves. But they are heavy to carry and they take up a lot of space. When I moved home last year I had six boxes to carry! Recently I bought an eReader. They are much lighter of course and they take up less space. In fact they don't take up any space at all. I have got rid of my six boxes of books and now I will only use the eReader. I already have about 50 books on the reader. It is more enjoyable to use than an ordinary book. It's fun! I like to use the dictionary on an eReader. If I see a word that I don't know I can find out the meaning by 'tapping' on the word. A dictionary definition then appears. With books, on the other hand, you have to find a dictionary and then look up the word that you want. It takes too much time and usually I don't bother. I will always use an eReader now, especially when travelling. They are much more convenient, but sometimes I do miss paper books.

8 **Complete the tables for Sam and Yoko comparing books and eReaders. Put a ✓ in the correct box.**

Sam	Books	eReaders	Yoko	Books	eReaders
lighter to carry		✓	lighter to carry		✓
easier to use			easier to use		
more enjoyable			more enjoyable		
less convenient for travelling			less convenient for travelling		

LANGUAGE: connecting words

We use connecting words such as *however, but, on the other hand* and *whereas* to join ideas that are contrasting. Put a circle around the connecting words in the following sentences:

a Exeter's winters are not very cold, **whereas** Edinburgh has cold and windy winters.

b Edinburgh has cold and windy winters. **On the other hand**, Exeter's winters are not very cold.

c Exeter's winters are not very cold, **but** Edinburgh has cold and windy winters.

d Edinburgh has cold and windy winters. **However**, Exeter's winters are not very cold.

 9 **Find the following connecting words in Sam and Yoko's paragraphs. Put a circle around them.**

however   but   on the other hand   whereas

 10 **Complete these sentences in your own words.**

a Istanbul and Ankara are very different cities. Istanbul is a very old city and is situated on the coast, whereas _____

b I'd like to visit Germany, but _____

c My father is trying to decide whether to leave England and go to work in Singapore. On the one hand, Singapore is a beautiful, modern place with good roads and high salaries. On the other hand, _____

d There's a new shopping mall near my house. However, _____

Sentence building

 11 **Look at the comparative sentences in the table below.**

What?	Verb	Adjective + ~er	*than*	What?	.
A keyboard	is	easier to use	than	a pen	.
Edinburgh	has	colder winters	than	Exeter	.
eReaders	are	lighter	than	books	.
a					
b					
c					
d					

Now add these sentences to the table. Put the words in the correct order first.

a London / Rome / has / than / summers / hotter

b juice / is / fresh / cola / healthier / than / fruit

c much taller / date / are / palms / than / palms / coconut

d prepare / an omelette / easier to / a boiled egg / than / is

12 **Look at these comparative sentences. They contain *more* or *less*.**

What?	Verb	*more/less*	Adjective	*than*	What?	.
Salalah's climate	is	more	comfortable	than	Muscat's climate	.
Word puzzles	are	less	interesting	than	computer games	.
An eReader	is	more	convenient to carry	than	a book	.
a						
b						
c						
d						

Now add these sentences to the table. Put the words in the correct order first.

a more / difficult / English / to learn / Chinese / than / is

b are / business letters / personal / email messages / than / less

c than / a smartphone / useful / less / an ordinary mobile / is

d is / silver / expensive / than / much more / to buy / gold

13 **Use these pictures to write comparative sentences. Follow this pattern:**

What?	Verb + ...	Adjective + ~er	*than*	What?	.
		more + **adjective**			

EXAMPLE: (wet) *London is wetter than Cairo.*

a (intelligent) _____

b (cheap) _____

c (beautiful) _____

d (good) _____

e (quick) _____

Joining ideas

LANGUAGE: *who* and *which* clauses – defining and non-defining

Read these sentences. They both contain *which* clauses. What is the difference between the two clauses?

a Moscow State University, **which is the largest university in Russia**, is situated on a hill overlooking Moscow.

b The university **which is the most suitable for your needs** is in St Petersburg.

Clause a just gives extra information about the college. It is **non-defining**.
Clause b tells us **exactly** which college the writer is writing about. It is **defining**.

Now look at these sentences. They both contain *who* clauses. Underline them. Which is defining and which is non-defining?

c The people who live next door are from Hong Kong.

d My neighbour, who is a teacher from Iran, has invited us all to his house tomorrow.

Note: In defining clauses it is possible to put *that* in place of *who* or *which*:

The university **that** is the most suitable for your needs is in St Petersburg.

The people **that** live next door are from Hong Kong.

14 **Read the letters from Kate and Aunt Sarah on pages 74–75. Read the paragraphs about books and eReaders on page 77.**

a Put a box around any *who, which* or *that* clauses.

b Which are defining? Which are non-defining? Write them in the table below.

Defining clauses (*which, who, that*)	Non-defining clauses (*which, who*)
which has the most suitable course	which I downloaded from Amazon

15 **Find the defining *who, which* or *that* clauses in these sentences. Underline them.**

a On our trip to India last year the place <u>which I liked best was Darjeeling</u>.

b Yesterday in the supermarket I saw the woman who reads the news on Channel 33.

c The exam which was planned for tomorrow has been postponed until next week.

d This is the car that I want to buy.

e The wadi that we visited for the field trip was one of the most interesting in Oman.

f People who study rocks are called geologists.

16 Match these sentences with the defining *which*, *who* or *that* clauses. Then write the sentences out in full in your notebook. Make sure you put the clause in the correct position in the sentence.

a That's the man.   ... that gets the best exam results

b We went to see the film and we liked it.   ... who we gave our order to

c The car is a bit too expensive.   ... that I would like to discuss in this lecture

d The waitress has disappeared.   ... that I would really like to buy

e The country is China.   ... which has the biggest population

f The college presents a prize to the student.   ... that I saw earlier today

g The topic is climate change.   ... which won all the Oscars

17 Look at the pictures below. Now complete the sentences with defining *which*, *who* or *that* clauses.

a That's the driver who/that _____ .

b The computer _____ has broken down.

c Paris is the city _____ .

d People _____ are known as 'fans' or 'supporters'.

Dictionary definitions

18 Look at these definitions.

> **economist** *noun* a person who is an expert in economics

a Underline the defining clause in the definition.

b Use your dictionary to help you write definitions for the following nouns in your notebook. Use defining *who*, *which* or *that* clauses.

> ~~a laptop computer~~   a taxi driver   a pilot   a doctor   a roof rack   an Internet browser

a laptop computer a portable computer that is suitable for use when travelling

Punctuation

> **LANGUAGE: commas and clauses**
>
> **Look at these sentences:**
>
> a   Jordan, which is famous for its historical sites, has become very popular with tourists.
> b   The historical site which attracts most tourists to Jordan is the ancient city of Petra.
>
> **Non-defining clauses (Sentence a) are placed between two commas or between a comma and a full stop. There are no commas before or after a defining clause (Sentence b).**

19   Some of these sentences need commas and some do not. Add commas where necessary.

a   Canberra which is the capital of Australia is not the biggest city in the country.

b   The shop had sold out of Jasmine Mystery which is my favourite perfume.

c   The man who robbed the bank was arrested yesterday.

d   The main course was sardines which are popular in Portugal.

e   Last week I wrote a letter to the college that I want to study in.

f   Yu Lin said she wanted to speak to the woman who was in charge of the shop.

g   The programme that I wanted to watch was cancelled at the last minute.

h   Peter who is a well-known journalist writes for a Cape Town newspaper.

i   All appointments have been cancelled by the president who has a slight stomach upset.

B Focus on the paragraph

Better paragraphs

Connecting words

1   Complete this passage with the words and phrases in the list.

> although   when   whereas   however   ~~on the one hand~~   who   which   but   less   more

Is life better now, or was life more rewarding in the past? **a** _On the one hand_ we have more material things nowadays, such as cars, mobile phones and computers. **b**_____ on the other hand, some people think that we were happier in the past, **c**_____ we had fewer possessions and life was **d**_____ complicated. My grandfather, for example, was a fisherman. He lived in a small village on the coast and had a very simple life. There was no electricity and the family had to bring water from a nearby well, **e**_____ they shared with the whole village. **f**_____ , I have never seen a man as happy as my grandfather.

Life is certainly **g**_____ comfortable nowadays. People **h**_____ live in cities have air-conditioning, hot and cold water and heating in the winter, **i**_____ in the old days these things were unheard of. One thing surprises me. **j**_____ we have all of these comforts at home, many people like to take a tent at the weekends and go camping in the desert. Perhaps they are looking for a simpler way of life.

Organization

It is important to organize a paragraph so that one idea follows from another logically. For example a paragraph may begin with a general statement:

There are many points in favour of nuclear power.

The paragraph then gives examples to support the statement:

For example, nuclear power is relatively cheap.

Remember, connecting words such as *first, second, although, on the other hand, also* show the organization of the paragraph and help the reader.

2 Read this introduction to an essay. What is the essay about?

The world's population is growing rapidly. We need more energy to supply new cities and industries. But how can we do this? Energy sources such as oil, gas and coal are limited. They will run out one day. Other sources such as water, wind and sun are possible, but at the moment they only produce small amounts of energy. Nuclear power is also an important source of energy. It is used in many countries, such as France and Japan. But is it safe and is it a good alternative to the other sources?

3 Put these sentences in the correct order to make two paragraphs.

A <u>There are many points in favour of nuclear power.</u>

a On the other hand, sources such as oil, gas and coal can cause a lot of damage to the environment. _____

b For example, nuclear power is a cheap source of energy. __1__

c It causes very little pollution, and also it requires very little mining, which can damage the environment. _____

d Secondly, nuclear power is also very good for the environment. _____

e The costs of running the power plant are very low, although the cost of building it is quite high. _____

B <u>However, there are many strong arguments against using nuclear power.</u>

f This waste is a by-product of nuclear plants and it is difficult to get rid of safely. _____

g For example, in 2011 a tsunami in Japan badly damaged nuclear power plants along the coast. _____

h First of all, there is the question of the safety. __1__

i There have been many serious problems with nuclear plants around the world. _____

j For these reasons many people are still not sure about nuclear power. _____

k Secondly, there is the problem of nuclear waste. _____

l It can remain radioactive for hundreds of years. _____

4   **Read the whole essay on page 83 again and choose a title.**

  a Different sources of energy   **b** Nuclear power in Japan
  c Nuclear power: for and against   **d** Safety problems with nuclear power

Style

> **LANGUAGE: style**
>
> **When we write we need to think about the reader.**
>
> Is the reader a friend, a teacher, an employer, a scientist, etc.?
> • We write in different styles for different readers.
> • We write in different styles for different types of text: emails, letters, essays, text messages, etc.
>
> **For friends we write informally. For example, we use:**
> • contractions (**you're** instead of **you are**)
> • shortened words (**TV** for **television**)
> • informal vocabulary (**chat** not **discussion**)
>
> **Note:** In text messages many people use symbols and abbreviations (lol, u, ☺, cul8r, bye).
> These should only be used in texting or chatting.

 5   **Answer these questions about style. Underline the correct answer.**

  a Who is the reader of the text about nuclear power?
      friend   scientist   general reader   teacher

  b Is the text ... ?
      very informal   informal   formal   very formal

  c Who is Kate writing to on page 74?
      friend   general reader   teacher   relative

  d Is Kate's letter ... ?
      very informal   informal   formal   very formal

6   **This letter is in response to an advertisement for a job. Underline the more formal options.**

Dear Sir,

I have seen your **advert / advertisement** for a trainee manager in the *New York Telegraph*.
The job sounds **very interesting / great** and I wonder if you could **give me / send me** details
of the job and an application form.

I'm / I am a student at the International University of Mexico. I will be leaving university
in the summer and I **would like to find / want to get** a job in catering. My first language is
Spanish, but I speak and write English **OK / quite well** and I also know **a little / a bit of** French.

I have **lots / a great deal** of experience in catering as I have worked in my uncle's restaurant
during the vacations. I also spent two months working in a hotel in Mexico City last
summer. It was a **really / very** useful experience.

I've got / I have some excellent references which I can send if **you want / you wish**.

Hoping to hear from you. / I look forward to hearing from you.

Yours faithfully, / Best wishes,

Free writing

7 **Francis lives in Manila, in the Philippines. He has a difficult decision to make. Read his letter to a magazine and write a reply in your notebook. Give him your advice. Begin your letter like this:**
Dear Francis,

> Some people think I am in a lucky position. Two companies have offered me jobs. One job is in my uncle's travel company in Manila, the other is with an airline company in Riyadh in Saudi Arabia. The money in Saudi Arabia is much better, and as the company is large the promotion prospects will be better. I have a wife and two children and they can come with me to Riyadh. The children will start primary school in September.
>
> On the other hand, I like my uncle very much and the work in his travel company will be interesting. I would have to arrange tours and accommodation for foreign tourists who are visiting the Philippines. Also, I could be near my parents if I stay in Manila. They are very old now and in poor health. However, I have to think about the future of my children too. What is best for them? What shall I do?
>
> *Francis*

8 **A friend is thinking of moving to Australia to work. He/she is planning to go either to Canberra or to Sydney. Write a paragraph in your notebook for your friend comparing the two cities. Use the information in the table. Add your own ideas and suggestions.**

	Canberra	Sydney
Description	Small modern city, capital of Australia, government the main employer, some light industry and tourism	Largest city in Australia, major port, the main industrial and commercial centre, beautiful harbour and beaches
Location	South-east Australia – inland, located on a river in an agricultural area	South-east Australia – located on Pacific coast
Climate	Cold and wet winters (sometimes snow) – warm and dry summers	Mild winters and warm summers
Population	Over 300,000	Over 3.5 million

9 **Read the paragraphs comparing books and eReaders on page 77. Now write a paragraph in your notebook comparing one of the following pairs:**

a emails or letters

b texting or phoning

c tablets or laptops

d TV or the Internet

Which do you prefer and why?

10 **Use comparatives and superlatives to write a paragraph in your notebook to compare the city, town or village you live in with the way it was in the past. How is the place different? Which things are better? Which things are worse?**

Use this checklist to edit your writing in Exercises 7–10.

CHECKLIST		EXERCISE		
	7	8	9	10
How many sentences are there?				
How many full stops (.) are there?				
Does every sentence begin with a capital letter?				
Does every sentence have a verb?				
Have you checked your spelling?				
Can you make your writing better?				

Editing

11   **Read this paragraph comparing two buildings. It is part of a report for a company that wants to rent a new building for offices. Find 15 mistakes in grammar and spelling. Then write the paragraph out in full in your notebook.**

There are two buildings which they are suitabel for the company. One is a building called Panorama House. It located close to the city centre in Station Road. The total area is 1,350sq m. It has six floors and a small reception area. Ther are six toilets and a small kitchen. From the sixth floor there are lovly views of the city. The second possibility is a bilding called Park Mansions, which it is much larger then Panorama House. It has eight floores. The reception area is biger too, wich it is very important for the company. Unfortunately the rent is more expensiver than the rent for Panorama House. It is $6,000 per month, wheras the rent for Panorama House is only $5,000. The location is less convenient too. Panorama House is more closer to the city centre.

12   **Edit the paragraph opposite that someone wrote for an encyclopaedia. There are no mistakes but the style is wrong. Write your corrected paragraph in your notebook.**

a   Find *two* examples of informal expressions that should be omitted.

b   Replace the underlined words and phrases with more formal items from the list below.
For example: *lots of = many*. You may need to change the order of the words in the sentences.

parallel   smaller   photos   for example   are called(x2)   is   a monocot   ~~many~~   i.e.   also   can be seen

FLOWERING PLANTS

There are ~~lots of~~ __many__ different types of plants, like ferns, conifers, and angiosperms. The largest group of plants are angiosperms, which we also call flowering plants. These plants produce flowers, which produce seeds and fruit. Well, flowering plants can be divided into two more types. These are known as monocots and dicots. The monocot, which, by the way, means 'one seed leaf', has got long narrow leaves. The veins in the leaves are all in the same direction. An example of one of these is the palm tree. On the other hand the dicot, that's to say, 'two-seeded leaf' has broader leaves. The veins are a bit different. There's a main vein and then there are little

veins branching off. A tomato plant is an example of a dicot. You can see these two types of angiosperm in the pictures.

monocot | dicot

Vocabulary building

Regular adjectives

 13 Complete this table. Make sure you spell the comparatives and superlatives correctly.

	Comparative	Superlative
cold	colder	coldest
hot		
big		
wet		
nice		
heavy		
dry		
easy		

Irregular adjectives

14 Complete this table with the correct form.

	good	bad	much/many	little	old
Comparative		worse	more		older
Superlative	the best			the least	

15 **Complete these facts with superlatives and the names in this list.**

> Al Azziziyah   Indonesia   ~~Baikal~~   Antarctica   Nile   Venezuela

a Lake Baikal _____ in Siberia is the world's _____ lake. It is more than 1,600m deep.

b The _____ river in the world is the _____ .

c _____ is the country with the _____ number of islands. There are more than 13,000.

d The _____ waterfall in the world is Angel Falls in _____ . It is 978m in height.

e The _____ place on Earth is _____ . The average temperature is -57.8°C.

f _____ in Libya is the _____ place on Earth. A temperature of 58°C was recorded there.

16 **Look at the questions below. The missing words are all long adjectives found in this unit. Write the answers in the puzzle below and find the vertical word. It is also an adjective.**

a I think the course at Harvard University is the most suitable _____ for you.

b This armchair is much more _____ than that wooden chair.

c The weather is _____ at the moment. It's not too hot and not too cold.

d I think letters are more _____ than emails.

e That book was very _____ . I'd like to read it again.

f Why don't you learn Spanish. It's less _____ than German.

g I like my old car, but it's not very _____ .

h The children said that they'd enjoyed *Star Wars*. It was very _____ .

i Einstein was one of the most _____ people who has ever lived.

▼

a __ __ __ __ __ __ __ __

b __ __ __ __ __ __ __ __ __ __ __

c __ __ __ __ __ __ __

d __ __ __ __ __ __ __ __

e __ __ __ __ __ __ __ __

f __ __ __ __ __ __ __ __ __

g __ __ __ __ __ __ __ __

h __ __ __ __ __ __ __ __

i __ __ __ __ __ __ __ __ __ __

Unit 5 Language review

A Comparatives

Remember there are two types of comparative adjective:				
Comparative: *~er than*		**Comparative: *more/less ... than***		
better worse bigger slower	than	less more	windy beautiful interesting modern	than

 1 **Put these words in the correct order to form a sentence. They all contain comparative forms.**

a by plane / better / by car / is / travelling / travelling / than

_____

b on a keyboard / easier / writing / than / with a pen / is

_____

c to learn / French / than / difficult / Chinese / more / is

_____

d in Germany / expensive / in Saudi Arabia / petrol / is / more / than / much

_____

e at work / the connection / at home / slower / is / my Internet connection / than

_____

f that / exciting / cricket / I think / a more / football / game / is / than

_____

g than / studying / interesting / at home / studying / less / at an overseas university / would be

_____

2 **Use the tourist information about two countries – A-land and B-land. Write sentences in your notebook comparing the two countries using the adjectives in brackets.**

	A-land	B-land
Hotels (comfortable)	★ ★ ★ ★ ★	★
Public transport (reliable)	★ ★ ★ ★ ★	★ ★
Winters (cold)	★ ★	★ ★ ★
Summers (wet)	★ ★ ★ ★ ★	★
People (friendly)	★ ★	★ ★ ★ ★ ★
Standard of living (good)	★ ★	★ ★ ★ ★ ★
Public safety (bad)	★ ★	★ ★ ★ ★
Scenery (beautiful)	★ ★ ★ ★ ★	★
Housing (expensive)	★ ★ ★	★ ★ ★ ★

B Superlatives

Superlatives: *the ~est*		Superlatives: *the most/the least ...*	
the	best	the most	suitable
	worst	the least	reliable
	biggest		beautiful
	coldest		interesting
	fastest		modern

  Put these words in the correct order to form a sentence. They all contain superlative forms.

a is made / the / silk / in China / best / in the world

_____

b metal / expensive / gold / most / is / the

_____

c was / to India / when we went / holiday / most / exciting / my

_____

d has / say / the / Vancouver / worst / some people / that / climate

_____

e interesting / one of / the / places / the Forbidden City / to visit / in China / most / is

_____

f is / least / car / I have owned / the / car / this / reliable

_____

g is / way / the / to get around / in a city / quickest / often / walking

_____

4 **Use the tourist information about three important cities – Ayeton, Beechester and Ceeville. Write sentences in your notebook comparing the three cities using the adjectives in brackets. Use superlative forms.**

	Ayeton	Beechester	Ceeville
Airport (busy)	★	★ ★ ★ ★ ★	★ ★ ★ ★
Population (large)	★ ★ ★	★ ★	★ ★ ★ ★ ★
Metro system (efficient)	★ ★ ★ ★ ★	★ ★ ★	★
Climate (good)	★	★ ★ ★ ★	★ ★
Streets (clean)	★ ★ ★	★ ★	★
Historic sites (interesting)	★ ★	★ ★ ★ ★ ★	★ ★ ★
Hotels (expensive)	★ ★ ★ ★ ★	★ ★	★ ★ ★
Restaurants (stylish)	★ ★	★ ★ ★ ★	★
Parks (attractive)	★ ★ ★ ★ ★	★	★ ★ ★ ★ ★
Traffic jams (bad)	★ ★ ★	★ ★ ★ ★ ★	★ ★

C *Who, which* and *that* clauses: defining and non-defining

Non-defining clauses: add *extra* information.

Kerala, **which is a state located in the south of India**, is sometimes called 'God's own country'.
Toni, **who is always absent from the class**, failed the exam and had to retake it.

Defining clauses: tell us *exactly* which person or thing the sentence is about.

Those students **who (that) were absent for the English exam**, can take it again next month.
Seattle is the city **which (that) became famous as the home of Microsoft and Starbucks**.

5 **Put these words in the correct order to form sentences. These sentences all contain defining clauses. Complete each sentence with your own ideas.**

a   most / was / enjoyed / I / which / last year / the film / _____

_____

b   is / that / admire / the person / I / in the world / most / _____

_____

c   _____ / to visit / I / like / is / would / the country / that / most

_____

6 **These sentences all contain non-defining clauses. Add commas where necessary. Try to solve the puzzle. Which country do these sentences describe?**

a   in the world / which / one of the largest / situated / in South America / is / is / this country

_____

b   of the country / is not / which / located / the capital / is / the biggest city / in the middle

_____

c   mainly Portuguese / who / speak / football and music / their love of / the people / are famous for

_____

The country is: _____

7 **Choose defining clauses from the list and add them to the sentences below.**

who was seen standing outside a bank   that we visited
who played the part of the king in the TV series   which I bought last week
that I wrote on the use of the Internet

a   The hospital was the oldest in the country.

_____

b   The car broke down on the motorway.

_____

c   The lecturer said he liked the report.

_____

d   The police are looking for a man.

_____

e   The actor died suddenly last week.

_____

8 **Choose non-defining clauses from the list and add them to the sentences below. Remember to add commas.**

which is opening next month
which is an island located in the Indian Ocean
who is one of the richest men in the world
which has a roof rack and an extra petrol tank
who is a famous Jamaican sprinter

a Usain Bolt is one of the most respected men in his sport.

_____

b The jeep is perfect for trips across the desert.

_____

c More than 400 students are expected to enrol at the New International University.

_____

d Bill Gates has decided to give most of his money away to charity.

_____

e Sri Lanka lies to the south of India.

_____

A Focus on the sentence

Looking at text

1 Samira is writing about her university. Read the text. Where is the university? How many students are there now?

I have been studying at the International University in Riyadh in Saudi Arabia for three years. I am a student in the Science faculty, and I study Maths, Chemistry and Physics. The university, which was built in 2008, is situated in a desert area about 25km from the centre of Riyadh. Since it was opened, the university has grown rapidly. It is now one of the biggest in Saudi Arabia.

In 2008 there were only 500 students, who mainly came from the area around Riyadh, and there were only three faculties, Law, Science and Humanities. In 2010, the number of students increased to 3,000 and two new faculties opened Education and Business. In 2012, the faculty of Information Technology was opened and the number of students grew to just over 6,000. Now the university has more than 12,000 students, who come from all over Saudi Arabia. The number of faculties has increased to nine.

The university campus has become more attractive during this time. Because the university had no trees or gardens in the early days, it used to be very dry and dusty. However, now there are gardens everywhere with fountains, flowers and hundreds of palm trees. We also have very good sports facilities. At the moment the authorities are building a new swimming pool.

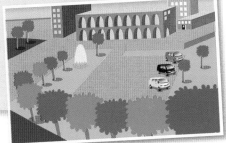

a Complete the graph showing student numbers.
b What has happened to student numbers between 2008 and now?

Between 2008 and now, student numbers _____

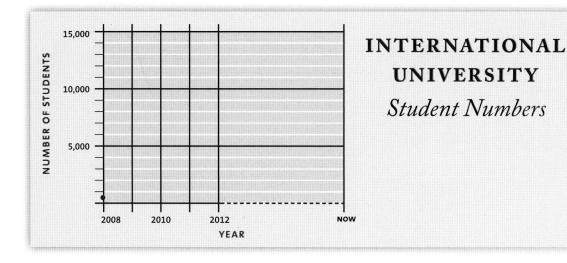

Answer these questions about the university.

a When was the university built?
The university was built in 2008.

b Where did the first students come from?

_____

c Where do they come from now?

_____

d Why was the campus dry and dusty at first?

_____

e Why is the campus more attractive now?

_____

LANGUAGE: past to present

Underline the verbs in these sentences. Then underline _for_ and _since_.

a Hizo has been studying at the college for six years.
b The students have been working hard for the past month.
c Our city has changed a lot since I was a boy.
d McDuncan's has built five new restaurants since 1998.

When we describe a period which continues from past to present we often use these verb forms:

have/has + ...~ed (_has changed, have studied_, etc.)
have/has + been + ...~ing (_has been studying, have been working_, etc.)

We often use these verbs with _for_ (_for six months, for ten minutes, for ages_) and _since_ (_since 1999, since Tuesday, since I was little_).

 Read about Samira's university again and answer these questions.

a Find _past to present_ verbs in Samira's text and underline them. How many are there?

_____

b Find a clause beginning with _since_ and underline it.

c Underline _which_ and _who_ clauses. How many are there? _____

d Find the phrase _used to be_ and underline it.

e Complete this sentence with your own words:
When I was little I used to _____

4   **Read this short article about the history of computers.**

THE HISTORY OF COMPUTERS_

Fifty years ago computers were so big that they filled a room. Nowadays <u>they</u> are placed on desks, carried in the pocket or even fitted into tiny instruments such as watches. They have been getting smaller and smaller because of improved technology. They have also been getting cheaper, which means that more people are able to own <u>one</u>. At the same time computers have been getting more powerful. The first computers could do just a few calculations in a second, whereas the modern microcomputer can do millions (a) _____ in a second. The first computer (b) _____ able to store a program, was built at Manchester University in 1948. This was a huge 'mainframe' computer. In 1960 the tiny silicon chip was invented, and because of <u>this</u> it became possible to build much smaller and faster computers. In the 1970s, the first desktop microcomputers appeared. Soon offices around the world had desktop computers. As computers became smaller they also became more portable. In 1981 the Osborne Computer Corporation introduced Osborne 1, the first portable computer. Although it was possible to carry <u>it</u>, it was still very heavy. It weighed 10.7 kg. Since <u>then</u>, however, portable computers, or laptops, have become much lighter and more compact. Sales (c) _____ have increased rapidly. Then in 2010 Apple introduced tablet computers, (d) _____ smaller and lighter than laptops. At the moment tablets and laptops are both very popular, but who knows what the future will be for computers.

a   Put these inventions in the correct order. Mark them on the timeline. The first has been done as an example.

A laptop	**B** silicon chip	**C** ~~mainframe computer~~	**D** the tablet	**E** the desktop

Past   C   **Now**

b   Complete the sentences below, which summarize the text. Use four words from this list:

slower	attractive	heavier	smaller	~~faster~~
expensive	larger	powerful	cheaper	interesting

For the last fifty years, computers have been getting _faster_____ , _____

and _____ . They have also become more _____ .

5 **Read the article again.**

a What do the underlined words refer to?

they _computers_   one _____

this _____   it _____

then _____

b Add these phrases to the article. The positions are marked a–d.

> which was   of computers   which were   of calculations

6 **Read about coffee production in Palania and complete the graph.**

The graph shows coffee production in Palania from 1995 up to the present day. During this period production levels have fluctuated greatly. In 1995 the total was 100,000 tonnes. This total increased steadily and reached a total of 150,000 tonnes in 2000. In 2001, however, there was a severe hurricane in the region, which destroyed many of the trees. Because of this, coffee production fell sharply that year to 120,000 tonnes. The following year production went up again, and by 2005 it reached 180,000 tonnes. However, in 2008 there was a collapse in the world coffee price. Too many countries were producing too much coffee and this caused the price to fall. As a result, many of the trees had to be destroyed in order to stop over-production of coffee. Production dropped to just under 100,000 tonnes in 2008 and remained at that level for the next two years. For the last few years, however, production has been increasing rapidly and the present total is just over 200,000 tonnes. The prospects for coffee production in the future are very good.

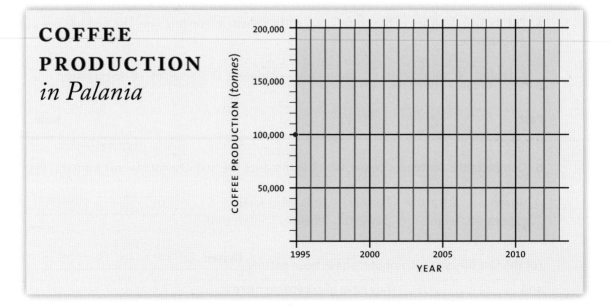

COFFEE PRODUCTION *in Palania*

LANGUAGE: time – past and past to present

Look. This is how we talk about:

- things that start and finish in the past (past simple, past continuous)
- things that start in the past and continue to the present (present perfect, present perfect continuous)

1 A point of time in the past (past simple)

2 A period in the past, now finished (past continuous)

3 A period starting in the past and continuing till now (present perfect/ present perfect continuous)

PRESENT

 Match the time diagrams with these six sentences.

a Since 1981 sales of computers have risen dramatically. ___3___

b Computers have been getting smaller and smaller. _____

c In 2001 there was a severe hurricane in the region. _____

d The campus has become more attractive during this time. _____

e Too many countries were producing too much coffee throughout 2008. _____

f This total increased steadily and reached a total of 150,000 tonnes in 2000. _____

8 **Read about coffee production again. Find examples of time types 1–3 and write them in your notebook.**

Sentence building

9 **Put these words in the correct order. Then write the sentences in the tables. They all describe past to present time using *since* or *for*.**

a since / bank / Maha / working / has / a / in / 2011 / been

b six o'clock / washing / their / have / the boys / car / been / since

c girl / Sarah / little / she / a / since / known / I / was / have

d many / family / kept / for / horses / has / years / my

e has / minutes / bus / for / for / a / twenty / Ali / waiting / been

f centuries / grown / the valley / people / rice / for / have / in

Who/what?	Verb	What?/Where?/How?	*since* + When	.
Carlos	has been studying	at the college	since last year	.
Coffee production	has gone down	rapidly	since the hurricane destroyed so many trees	.
a				
b				
c				

Who/What?	Verb	What?/Where?/How?	*for* + How long	.
Maria	has been working	at United Cosmetics	for six months	.
Fatima and her family	have lived	in Doha	for two years	.
d				
e				
f				

10 Write sentences like those in Exercise 9. Write three with *since* and three with *for*.

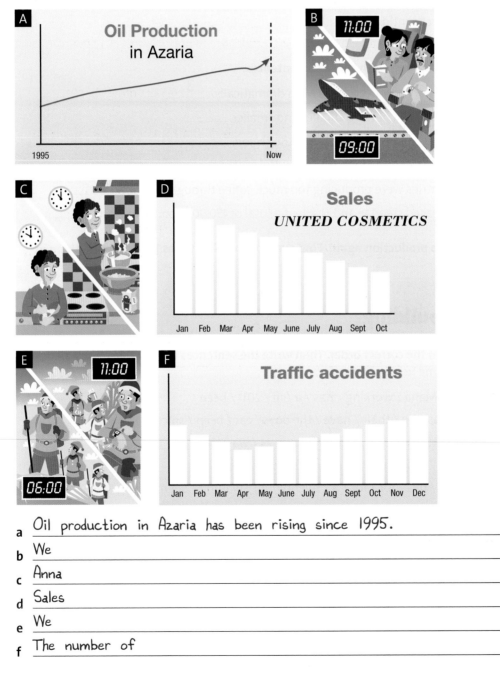

a Oil production in Azaria has been rising since 1995.

b We

c Anna

d Sales

e We

f The number of

11 Write four sentences in your notebook about yourself or people you know.
Use past to present verbs with *for* and *since*.

Joining ideas

LANGUAGE: *because* clauses

A *because* clause tells us *why* something happened. It can come at the beginning or the end of a sentence.

First part of the sentence	*Because* clause
The campus was dry and dusty in the early days	because it had no trees or gardens.

Because clause	Last part of the sentence
Because it had no trees or gardens,	the campus was dry and dusty in the early days.

Remember: a *because* clause is a clause not a sentence. It must be joined to a sentence.

 12 **Match these sentences. Then join each pair to make one sentence using *because*. Write the sentences in your notebook.**

1 Keiko is studying Business Studies, English and Computing.

2 Coffee production fell dramatically last year.

3 More and more people are buying computers.

4 Nina couldn't come to the birthday party yesterday.

5 The government is building ten new schools.

6 Boris has been trying to save money for the last six months.

a They are becoming cheaper and cheaper.

b She was taking an examination at the college.

c He wants to go on holiday to San Francisco in the summer.

d Many trees were destroyed by bad weather.

e The population of the country has been increasing rapidly in recent years.

f He wants to work for a large multinational company.

Keiko is studying Business Studies, English and Computing because he wants to work for a large multinational company.

13 **Complete these sentences with *because* clauses. Write the sentences out in full in your notebook.**

EXAMPLE: *We are not going out today ... because it is raining*

a Sarah decided to buy a new phone ...

b Elena got excellent marks in the examination ...

c Ali couldn't watch the film on television yesterday ...

d Hari has been working very hard since the beginning of the year ...

e The price of bananas has gone up recently ...

f The road through the mountains has been closed for two days ...

LANGUAGE: *because of this/as a result*

We can show *why* something happened by using a *because* clause:

The campus was dry and dusty **because it had no trees or gardens.**

We can also link the ideas in two sentences by using connecting words, for example:

because of this
as a result

These connectors link the cause and the effect.

CAUSE

EFFECT

Ali left the gate open when he went out. **Because of this**, the sheep ate all of his vegetables.

Ali left the gate open when he went out. **As a result**, the sheep ate all of his vegetables.

 14 Read about coffee production on page 96 again.

a Find two sentences beginning with *because of this* and *as a result*. Write them on the lines below.

_____

_____

b Complete these sentences in your own words.

My brother left his airline ticket at home. As a result, _____

_____

Sales of cars fell sharply last month. Because of this, _____

_____

There has been no rain for the last six months. Because of this, _____

_____

There was no electricity in the school yesterday. As a result, _____

_____

c Write two examples of your own using *as a result* and *because of this*.

_____

_____

_____

_____

_____

Clauses

15 In the table below are some of the clauses we have studied in *Better Writing*.
Add these parts of sentences to the table.

a we decided to cancel the trip to Fujaira.

c we decided to make the trip to Fujaira.

e you can connect your smartphone to
   the Internet.

b the juice is extracted from the fruit.

d many new trees had to be planted.

f there was just one office and three
   employees.

Clause	Last part of the sentence
When the business started,	f
As the machine spins around,	
In order to increase coffee production,	
If there is WiFi in a coffee shop,	
Although the weather was bad,	
Because the weather was bad,	

16 Remember *who* and *which* clauses? Look at the *who* and *which* clauses in these two sentences.
They are non-defining (they just give extra information).

EXAMPLE: *The university, which* was built in 2008, *is situated in a desert area about* 25km from the city.
Now the university has more than 12,000 students, who come from many different countries.

Complete these sentences with *who* or *which* clauses.

a The mathematics teacher, who _____ , has been teaching
   since 2000.

b The Giza pyramids, which _____ , are popular with tourists
   from all over the world.

c Nelson Mandela, who _____ , died in 2013.

d I received a letter from a friend of mine called Mike, who _____ .

e Last summer my family visited Istanbul, which _____ .

f Hummus, which _____ , is quite easy to prepare.

LANGUAGE: reduced clauses

Look at the sentences below. They all contain defining clauses.

The car **which is parked near the tree** belongs to my cousin.
The car **parked near the tree** belongs to my cousin.

The words *which is* are omitted in the second sentence. There is no difference in meaning.
... parked near the tree **is called a** *reduced clause.*

Now look at this pair of sentences:

The man **who is managing the factory** is called Peter Yu.
The man **managing the factory** is called Peter Yu.

The words *who is* are omitted in the second sentence. There is no difference in meaning.
... managing the factory **is a reduced clause.**

17 Reduce these defining clauses. Write the sentences in full on the lines below.

EXAMPLE: *The first computer ~~which was~~ able to store a program was built at Manchester University in 1948.*

The first computer able to store a program was built at Manchester University in 1948.

a The man who is wearing a brown jacket is a chemistry professor.

_____

b The tall tower that is built like a rocket is the Holiday Hotel.

_____

c The president is the short, fat man who is speaking to the old lady.

_____

d The country that is most famous for growing coffee is Brazil.

_____

e Andrea Bocelli is a blind Italian singer who is known for his wonderful voice.

_____

Punctuation

18 Correct this paragraph about changes in aeroplanes. Add capital letters, full stops and commas where necessary. Then write the paragraph out in full in your notebook.

aeroplanes have been getting bigger and faster over the years the first modern aeroplane was the boeing 247 which was introduced in 1933 it had room for 10 passengers during the second world war the jet engine was developed the first jet airliner which was called the comet started service in 1952 it had four jet engines and could fly at 885kph later in 1958 pan american airlines introduced the boeing 707 which could carry 112 passengers because of the powerful engines the plane was able to cross the atlantic from new york to london in less than eight hours which was half the time of the old propeller aircraft

B Focus on the paragraph

Better paragraphs

Style

 1 **Read Sarah's email message to her English teacher in the university.**

a What style do you think the message is in – very formal, formal, informal or very informal?

b Find three things in the message that are typical of this style.

_____   _____   _____

c Add the following clauses to the email. Check your answers and then write the message out in full in your notebook.

> If I needed help
>
> who is a friend of my father's
>
> because I was late for class
>
> if it's not too hot
>
> which has been rather boring
>
> which is just outside my bedroom window
>
> who's not working at the moment
>
> As I was running down the stairs from the first floor to the ground floor

Dear Mrs Fernandez,

I am writing this email to you from my bed. I broke my leg badly three weeks ago on the stairs in the university. I was in a hurry. I slipped and fell to the bottom. I felt a terrible pain in my left leg and I couldn't move. At the hospital the doctor told me that my leg was broken. After resetting my leg in plaster, he said that I should rest at home for at least a month and then come back to see him. He told me to phone him. Since then I've been at home. I've been getting better bit by bit. I've been reading my course books and surfing the Internet, but I can't wait until I can walk again. Sometimes I sit in the garden. My older sister has been looking after me. She's been wonderful!

I'm sorry I am missing your classes. I'll let you know when I can return to the university.

Best wishes,

Sarah

Organization

2 This paragraph is about sugar production in Azaria. Put these sentences in the correct order (the first and last sentences are already in position). Use the connecting words and other clues to help you. Then write the paragraph out in full in your notebook.

SUGAR PRODUCTION IN AZARIA

In 2000 the amount of raw sugar produced in Azaria was 6.5 million tonnes. This total made the country one of the largest producers of sugar in the world.

a Then, in 2010, there was a very poor sugar harvest due to very dry conditions all through the year. _____

b However, at the end of the war, in 2004, production started to improve steadily. _____

c It remained at this low level for the next three years as the war continued. _____

d Since 2010 there has been plenty of rainfall every year but production has not risen greatly. _____

e Farm workers were needed in the army and as a result sugar production fell sharply that year to less than 3 million tonnes. _____

f It reached 5.5 million tonnes in 2007 and stayed at this high level for the next two years. _____

g However, the following year, 2001, a war began with the Pandoran Republic. ____1_____

h Crops in many areas died because of a lack of water and as a result production fell to just under 4 million tonnes in that year. _____

It now stands at around 4.5 million tonnes, well below the total of the year 2000.

Use information from the paragraph to complete the graph.

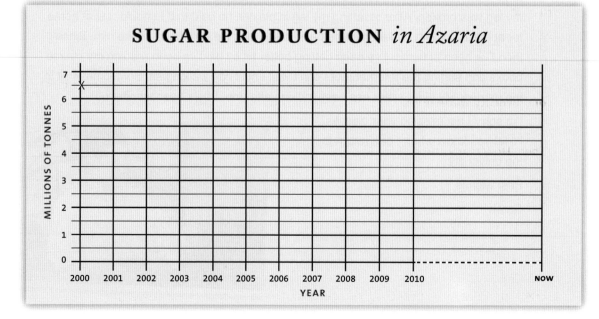

Connecting words

3 Read this passage about shopping. Add these connecting words and phrases:

> however also since although because which
> because of this whereas which ~~but~~

In the past shopping was a social occasion. People used to go to their local market not only to buy food and other goods,

a _____**but**_____ also to find out what was going on in their community. Each shop or market stall sold a particular product – fruit, vegetables, meat, perfumes, soap, cloth, etc. b_____ a shopping trip took a long time. People went from shop to shop chatting with the shopkeeper and discussing everything from prices to politics.

c_____ , in the 1950s and 1960s there were great changes in the lifestyles of many people. More and more people had a refrigerator, d_____ meant it was possible to store fresh food at home. More and more people were e_____ able to afford cars. f_____ then shops have increased in size and have become more and more centralized. g_____ in the past we bought things from many different shopkeepers, we now shop in large department stores, supermarkets and shopping malls, h_____ sell everything under one roof. We no longer have to worry about the weather. People drive to these centres and load up their cars with goods. i_____

people have refrigerators and freezers, they can buy all the food they need for weeks. j_____ shopping has become easier and more pleasant, it has also become less personal. It is now possible to buy everything you need in a supermarket or department store without chatting to anyone.

Free writing

4 Read about the International University on page 93. Find information about *your* school, college or university. Make notes in the space below.

Where are you studying? _____   When was it opened? _____

Then: How many students were there? What was it like?

_____

_____

Now: How many students are there now? What changes have there been?

_____

_____

Use your notes to write a paragraph about the place where you are studying.

5 **Look at this graph. It shows coffee production in Azaria since 2000.**
Write a paragraph in your notebook to describe the graph.

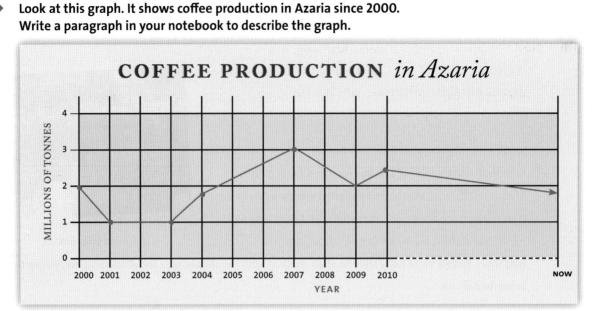

COFFEE PRODUCTION *in Azaria*

6 **Read the passage about computers on page 95 again. Now look at this information about the changes in cars since 1907. Write a paragraph in your notebook to describe the changes.**

Cars

1907	First cheap car – the Model T
1938	Volkswagen Beetle – very popular
1950s	Bigger and bigger cars (e.g., Cadillac)
1970s	Increase in fuel costs
Since 1970s	Smaller, more economical cars
Now	400 million in the world Cars are more comfortable, faster, safer and more economical

7 **Write a letter to a friend. Describe something that has happened to you recently. Describe the changes it has made to your life. (For example you have a new job, you have moved to a new house or flat, you have started a new course of study, etc.) Use your notebook.**

Use this checklist to edit your writing in Exercises 4–7.

CHECKLIST	EXERCISE			
	4	5	6	7
How many sentences are there?				
How many full stops (.) are there?				
Does every sentence begin with a capital letter?				
Does every sentence have a verb?				
Have you checked your spelling?				
Can you make your writing better?				

Editing

8 **Read this paragraph about global warming. It is part of an essay.**

a Correct spelling and grammatical mistakes. There are 11 mistakes.

b Look at the pairs of underlined sentences. How can we join these pairs of sentences together with connecting clauses?

c Check your answers and write the paragraph out in full in your notebook.

Global warming is caused by an increse in the amount of carbon dioxide in the Earth's atmosphere. (1) <u>Carbon dioxide are produced naturally by vegetation. It is important part of the atmosphere</u>. It traps the sun's heat. It warms the surface of the Earth. Normally there is a balance between the gases in the atmospher. In recent years the amount of carbon dioxide has went up. This is because of the burning of fossil fuels and the destruction of forests. (2) <u>The temperature of the Earth's surface have been going up. These has meant changes in Earth's climate</u>. (3) <u>Many parts of the world are becoming hoter and drier. Other parts are experiencing more storms and rainfall</u>. Sea level it has also been riasing. This is because the polar ice-caps have been melting.

Vocabulary building

Describing change

9 **Divide these verbs into two groups: verbs which mean the same as increase, and verbs which mean the same as decrease. Write them in the lists below.**

go down go up fall ~~grow~~ improve collapse rise ~~drop~~

increase

grow_____

_____

_____

_____

decrease

drop_____

_____

_____

_____

Faculties and subjects

10 **Find the names of these subjects.**

a c H E M I S T R Y   b P _ _ _ _ _ _ S   c _ I O _ _ _ _ _

d H _ _ _ O _ _   e _ _ _ _ G R _ _ _ _ _

f M _ _ _ _ M _ _ _ _ _ S g C _ _ P _ _ _ _ S C _ _ _ _ _

Add other subjects to the list.

_____

11 **Find the names of these faculties.**

a s C I E N C E   b L _ _   c E D _ _ _ _ _ _ _ _

d A _ _ S   e E N _ _ _ _ _ _ _ _ G

Add other faculties to the list.

_____

Use these clues to complete the crossword below.

Across

1 Aeroplanes have been ____ bigger and faster. (7 letters)

5 Farida has to rest ____ her broken leg is better. (5)

7 In the past people shopped in markets. ____ many people shop in department stores and supermarkets. (8)

11 Supermarkets are very convenient for shoppers. ____ the other hand, they are less personal than markets. (2)

12 The way out of a room or building is the ____. (4)

13 After picking, dates are ____ in the sun. (5)

16 Jericho, ____ is the oldest city in the world, is situated in the Jordan valley. (5)

18 What will happen to the price of oil next year? Will it rise ____ will it fall? (2)

19 My cousin has been in secondary school ____ two years. (3)

20 I've been ____ to save money since the beginning of the semester. (6)

22 The university authorities ____ building a new mosque on the campus. (3)

24 Computers have become smaller and more powerful. They have ____ become cheaper. (4).

26 The Mumtaz Hotel, which has been ____ for three months, is going to open again on Saturday. (6)

28 The population is rising rapidly. ____ a result, several more schools will be needed in the future. (2)

29 Because there were ____ trees or gardens, the campus was very dusty. (2)

30 'Are you going to feed the sheep?' 'No, I ____ them half an hour ago.' (3)

Down

1 Production of raw sugar has ____ down steadily since 1989. (4)

2 Is that the dress ____ you want to buy? (4)

3 Modern computers can do millions of calculations ____ a second. (2)

4 Farida has been feeling bored ____ she broke her leg. (5)

5 We ____ to go to Turkey every summer but now we go to London. (4)

6 In order ____ stop over-production of coffee, many trees had to be destroyed. (2)

8 ____ is another name for a cow or bull. (2)

9 The campus is very attractive, ____ many trees, flowers and fountains. (4)

10 ____ the weather forecast was rather bad, we decided to go on a picnic. (8)

14 If global warming continues, sea levels will ____ all over the world. (8)

15 From 2010–2013 the production of coffee ____ from 8 million tonnes to 6.5 million. (7)

16 Mumbai is a port on the Indian Ocean, ____ Delhi is located inland hundreds of miles from the coast. (7)

17 Since ____ was opened, the college has grown rapidly. (2)

19 Farida ____ down some stairs and broke her leg. (4)

21 Almost every office desk has ____ own PC. (3)

23 Port Sudan is situated on the ____ Sea. (3)

25 Last summer we went ____ holiday to Beirut. (2)

27 Tokyo is one ____ the biggest cities in the world. (2)

Unit 6 Language review

A Past to present

Remember we use the present perfect tense when describing
actions which start in the past and continue to the present.

Present perfect

	Past participle
have
has	changed
studied
risen
been

My country **has changed** a lot over the last 20 years.

1 In 1970 Abu Dhabi was a small coastal village. Now it is a large city. These sentences describe the
changes. Complete the sentences by putting the verb into the present perfect form.

a The population of Abu Dhabi _____ (increase) dramatically since 1970.

b There _____ (be) a big rise in the number of cars.

c People _____ (come) from all over the world to live in Abu Dhabi.

d The government _____ (build) many new schools and hospitals for the
growing population.

e The oil and gas industries _____ (grow) rapidly since 1970.

f Many large companies _____ (set up) offices in Abu Dhabi.

g Tourism _____ (go up) sharply during this period.

h Many new roads and bridges _____ (be built) in recent years.

We can also use the continuous form of the present perfect to talk about
'past to present' time. We use this to emphasize that the action is still continuing.

Present perfect continuous

		~ing
have
has	been	studying
rising
falling

You are late! I **have been waiting** for half an hour.

2 **Complete these sentences with verbs in the present perfect continuous form.**

a Lee _____ (work) in an electronics company for six years.

b My little brother _____ (play) computer games all day.

c I _____ (learn) to play the piano since I was little.

d The price of gold _____ (fall) recently.

e We _____ (live) in America since 2005.

f How long _____ you _____ (study) at the university?

g My grandfather _____ (drive) for 40 years and he has never had an accident.

h I'm sorry I'm late. _____ you _____ (wait) long?

3 **Put these words in the correct order to form a sentence. They all contain present perfect or present perfect continuous forms.**

a years / the same / twenty / worked / Professor Lee / for / university / in / has

_____

b two / nearly / talking / the phone / has / Maria / for / hours / been / on

_____

c grown / recent / Kuala Lumpur / years / rapidly / has / in

_____

d has / ten o' clock / in the oven / roasting / the chicken / since / been

_____

e have / your relatives / how / in China / been / long / living / ?

_____

f since / studied / Tony / he / French / to Paris / has / moved

_____

B *Because* clauses

A *because* clause tells us *why* something happened. It can come at the beginning or the end of the sentence. Notice the position of the comma.

The town is completely flooded	**because it rained heavily last week.**
Because it rained heavily last week,	the town is completely flooded.

4 **Complete these sentences in your own words. They all contain *because* clauses.**

a _____ because I want to become an engineer.

b Because I stayed up late to watch a programme on TV, _____ .

c Because there was a sharp fall in the company's profits last month,

_____ .

d _____ , because traffic jams in the capital were getting worse.

e _____ , because my father got a job overseas.

C *Because of this/As a result*

Because of this and *As a result* are connectors (like *However*, *On the other hand*, *Then*, etc.).
They show a link between a *cause* and an *effect*.

Cause	Effect
The farmer left the gate open.	**Because of this**, the sheep ate all his vegetables. **As a result**, the sheep ate all his vegetables.

5 **Match the causes and effects in the table below. Write sentences in your notebook using *Because of this* or *As a result*.**

Cause	Effect
a The team's best player was sick last week.	Many people ran out into the street.
b Hari's computer broke down last night.	More and more people can afford to buy them.
c The government has increased the price of petrol.	Motorists are feeling very upset.
d The building started to shake a few hours ago.	This afternoon's cricket match has been cancelled.
e It has been raining since early this morning.	They played badly and lost an important match.
f The price of laptops has been falling over the last few years.	He was unable to hand in the assignment on time.

D Reduced clauses

Defining clauses can often be reduced.

The car **which is parked near the tree** belongs to my cousin.
The car **parked near the tree** belongs to my cousin.

  Underline the relative clauses in these sentences. Reduce the clauses as in the example above.

a The doctor who is treating my father is very well qualified.

_____

b Yesterday we went to the Chinese restaurant that is mentioned in all the guide books.

_____

c The factory which was closed down last winter will reopen next month.

_____

d Each year the teacher who is voted the best by all the students is given a prize by the headmaster.

_____

e The person who I admire most in all the world is Barack Obama.

_____

f The computer that I want to buy is too expensive for me at the moment.

_____

E Clauses

In this book we have studied these clauses:

When ... , As ... , If ... , Although ... , Because ... , Who ... , Which ... , That ...

Remember clauses cannot stand alone. They are attached to a main clause.

Main clause	(Dependant) Clause
The fisherman went out to sea	although the weather was bad.

7 **Add these clauses to the sentences below.**

> who comes from Toulouse in south-west France
>
> that my brother bought
>
> when I first saw the university campus
>
> as the price of the product rises
>
> which we carried out last semester
>
> if I had as much money as Bill Gates
>
> because there weren't enough students
>
> although the climb was very difficult in places

a _____ , we managed to reach the top of the mountain before midday.

b The course in architecture had to be cancelled, _____ .

c _____ , I knew I would be happy studying there.

d Sales usually fall _____ .

e The new director of the college, _____ , called a meeting for all the staff.

f The survey, _____ , showed that most students preferred to study at home and not in the library.

g The car _____ had to go to the garage after just one week.

h _____ , I would also give it to charity.

To the teacher

While *Better Writing* includes a lot of work at the sentence level, the main focus is on the paragraph. Students move on from accuracy to writing fluency, and from mechanical skills (capitalization, spelling, punctuation) to the skills required to write longer stretches of text. The aim is make students aware of what 'better' writing involves: that is, writing which is more cohesive, better organized, more appropriate to the reader and easier to read – as well as writing which is more accurate.

How is grammar approached?

Though this book is not a grammar course, items of grammar are dealt with where appropriate. The range of grammatical structures used includes the present passive, reported speech forms and the present and past perfect tenses. Grammatical terminology is kept to a minimum. The structure of a sentence is explained as far as possible through a simplified teaching grammar, using terms such as *Who? How? Which? What?* and *When?* Students are, however, expected to be familiar with basic grammatical terms such as *adjective, noun, verb, clause, passive* and *past participle*.

What is the sequence through a unit?

Each unit follows a similar format, starting from a *Looking at text* section focusing on how specific language items are being used in context, through to a *Free writing* section towards the end of the unit, where students produce their own paragraphs. In between, there are a number of activities where students are asked to manipulate language, rearrange sentences or complete guided paragraphs.

The main steps followed through each unit are:

Looking at text This section contains a number of reading texts which illustrate the functional area of the unit and serve as a model for later free writing. The activities based on the texts are designed to raise the student's awareness of features within them, whether language structures or organizational and cohesive features.

Sentence building Tables are used to make the structure of sentences clear. Students are asked to reorder words in sentences and to complete tables.

Joining ideas Here the focus is mainly on the use of clauses to join ideas and shorter sentences in order to produce more cohesive writing.

Punctuation Exercises in this section focus on the use of capital letters, commas, full stops, speech marks, apostrophes, etc.

Better paragraphs Guided activities focus on the organization and cohesion of paragraphs.

Free writing In this section students use the paragraphs in *Looking at text* as models to write their own texts. Notes, diagrams and pictures are used to give students guidance.

Editing Students develop the habit of checking their written work through editing exercises which focus not only on spelling, grammar and punctuation, but also on how clauses and connectors can be used to improve writing.

Vocabulary building A variety of activities are used to review the vocabulary areas of the unit. Students improve their vocabulary-learning techniques by a) organizing words into content areas, b) using illustrations to facilitate learning and c) learning collocations of new words.

Language review This section focuses on the main language items which have featured in the unit, for example – clauses, tenses, dimensions and the use of articles. It gives additional practice in these areas.

How should the course be taught?

This depends on the students and teacher. Four different approaches are possible:

1 **Teacher led** The class is kept at roughly the same point in the course. The teacher introduces each section of the unit and checks progress.

2 **Group work** In a multi-level class students can be divided into small groups according to writing ability. Groups work through the units together. The teacher can then give greater attention to weaker students.

3 **Individual work** Students work through the book at their own pace. The teacher monitors progress and checks work during the lesson. However, it is recommended that this approach is adopted only when students are familiar with the structure of the units.

4 A combination of the above methods

Should students write in the book?

Gap-fill exercises can be completed in the book if this is acceptable, but for the sake of clarity and encouraging good writing habits, sentence and paragraph writing should be done in notebooks or, where available, on the computer. Writing can also be produced on single sheets or posters for wall displays on themes such as *How things work, How things are made* or *Comparison* (of cities, countries, etc.).

Answer key

Unit 1 A

1 jeep = Salah, watch = Yoko, phone = Maria, sailboat = Tony

2 **b** 's = has, 've = have

3 Students' own answers

4 wide–width, high–height, thick–thickness

5 Students' own answers

6 D

7 **a** consists of
b are white, are blue
c is, is small
d are used for

8 **a** Our boat has got a small engine at the back.
b My little radio has got one speaker on each side.
c These shirts have got two pockets at the front.
d Many laptops have got a disk drive on the right.

9 **a** The Japanese flag has got a red circle in the middle.
b The camera (This camera) has got a viewfinder on the top.
c The bus has got advertisements on the side.

10 **a** There is a red circle in the middle of the Japanese flag.
b There is a viewfinder on the top of the camera.
c There are advertisements on the side of the bus.

11 **a** A credit card is made of plastic.
b A knife is made of metal.
c Envelopes are made of paper.
d Tyres are made of rubber.
e A credit card is used for paying for goods and services.
f A knife is used for cutting things.
g Envelopes are used for sending letters.
h Tyres are used for covering wheels.

12 **a** The jeep is new with tinted windows and power steering.
b The watch is oval with silver hands and a gold strap.
c The phone is small with large, luminous numbers.
d The boat is green with a white mast and a red sail.

13 Students' own answers

14 I use my phone when I go shopping.
My brother uses the car when he goes camping in the desert.

15 Students' own answers

16 When visitors come to Kuwait, they should take a trip to Kuwait towers.
When you go up in the lift, you can see the whole of Kuwait.

17 It's got a memory, but it hasn't got a brain. It's rectangular in shape and quite thin. It looks like a briefcase and is about the same size. It's very easy to carry as it is made mostly of plastic and only weighs about 2kg. When you open the lid, you find a screen and a keyboard inside. People use these machines when they are travelling. What is it?

a 7 sentences **b** laptop computer

Unit 1 B

1 **a** A = 10, B = 5 **b** It (line 1), She (line 2), with (line 3), and so I wear it when (line 5)
c Students' own answers

2 **a** and **b** with **c** It **d** when **e** There
f so **g** got **h** also **i** when **j** it

3 **a** horse **b** made **c** rectangular **d** long **e** wide
f height **g** weighs **h** There **i** got **j** shield

4 Students' own answers

5 Students' own answers

6 Students' own answers

7 Students' own answers

8 It **has** got four legs, but it can't walk. It **is** rectangular in shape and there is a leg at each corner. It measure**s** about a metre in **height**. **The** top is 1.8m long and 70cm **wide** and has a thickness of 4cm. Ours is made **of** wood, but sometimes they are made of plastic or **glass**. In our house we keep it in the dining **r**oom.
It's a table.

9 *Suggested answer*:

My friend Hassan has got a new radio. He bought it a few days ago. It is black with a red handle. Hassan likes the radio very much. It is very light so he can take it everywhere. When he has a shower, he takes the radio with him.

10 very small, quite small, small, not very big, quite big

11 **a** black **b** white **c** blue **d** red
e yellow **f** green **g** pink

12 Students' own answers

13 **A** rectangular, **B** square, **C** oval, **D** round, **E** long, **F** thin

14 **a** bad **b** not very good **c** quite good
d good **e** very good **f** excellent

Unit 1 Language review

1 Students' own answers

2 Students' own answers

3 Students' own answers

4 Students' own answers

5 Students' own answers

6 **a** Sami often plays football when he has free time.
b We always take plenty of food when we go on a picnic.
c The examiner collects all the papers when the exam finishes.
d When the clock stops you must change the batteries.
e When the weather becomes very hot we always use air-conditioning.
f When Maria wants to relax she usually listens to her favourite music.

7 Students' own answers

Unit 2 A

1 **A** base station, **B** mobile switching centre, **C** cell

2 The phone sends a signal. The kettle heats water. The washing machine washes clothes. My phone can store 200 numbers. A signal is sent to the phone. Electricity is produced by the sun. The computer must be protected by a password. Some cars are powered by batteries.

3 **d** this = a base station,
there = mobile switching centre

4 **a** someone living in the house
b the caller

5 Students' own answers

6 **a** Switch on the answering machine when you go out.
b Leave a message after the 'bleep'.
c Press the 'play' button when you want to listen to your messages.
d Plug in the machine before you begin.
e Check the user's manual when you have a problem.
f Press the delete button after listening to the messages.
g Don't use the machine before you have read the instructions.

8 **a** *Passive verbs*:
is made, is guaranteed,
must be washed, should be peeled and cut,
is switched on, are pushed, is separated, is collected

b 1A, 2D, 3E, 4B, 5C, 6F
c 1 – A (washed), 2 – D (peeled), 3 – E (cut),
4 – B (switched on), 5 – C (pushed), 6 – F (collected)

9 **c** remove the lid, clean out the container, remove the jug, pour the juice

10 **a** The MP3 player folder is opened on the PC.
b The music is copied from the PC onto the MP3 player.
c The MP3 player is removed from the PC.
d The headphones are fitted to the MP3 player.
e The headphones are placed over the ears.
f The 'play' button is pressed.
g The volume can be adjusted as required.

11 **a** Open the MP3 player folder on the PC.
b Copy the music from the PC onto the MP3 player.
c Remove the MP3 player from the PC.
d Fit headphones to the MP3 player.
e Place the headphones over the ears.
f Press the 'play' button.
g Adjust the volume as required.

12 **a** Singapore is linked to Malaysia by a causeway.
b Trees and bushes are planted in the forest.
c The mobile phone is connected to a charger.
d The garage door is opened by a remote control unit.

13 **a** The vegetables are peeled and cut into small pieces.
b The signal is sent to an aerial and then transmitted to a telephone exchange.
c The phone is made of plastic and the case made of leather.
d The outgoing message is recorded and the machine switched on.
e The juice is poured into a jug and stored in a refrigerator.
f The clothes are taken out of the machine when the cycle is finished and put outside to dry.

14 As the machine spins around, juice is separated from the pulp.

15 **A** As the hot lava flows down the volcano, vegetation and houses may get destroyed.
B As the air rises over the hills, clouds form and rain may fall.
C As the climbers go higher up the mountain, the amount of oxygen in the air decreases.
D As the hurricane gets close to land, large waves may form.

16 If your friend's phone is outside the range of the network then you cannot make the call.

17 **A** If the trees start to die, they should be removed and replaced with new ones.
B If you have no Internet connection, please call our helpline to speak to a computer engineer.
C If the car overheats, wait for the engine to cool and then add water.
D If the fire alarm sounds, staff must use the stairs to leave the building and not the lift.

18 *Possible answers*:
   b leave the house
   c have any difficulties with their bookings
   d board the bus
   e feel ill
   f you board the plane

19 In order to make a phone call, the required number is keyed in.
   To clean the pulp from the extractor, the lid must be removed.
   In order to record the outgoing message, speak into the microphone.
   To take good photographs, the amount of light must be measured.

20 **a** The books belong to one student.
   b The books belong to more than one student.
   c The secretary is ill.
   d The secretary has got a fever.

21 **a** The dog's got some bad cuts on its leg.
   b I'm afraid the radio's broken.
   c No change.
   d It's situated at the top of a hill.
   e There's a flag at the top of the building.
   f No change.
   g The machine's switched off at the moment.
   h Five teachers have their desks in this room.
   It's called the teachers' room.

22 **a** **If the caller is in an underground car park,** it may be impossible to use the mobile phone.
   b **When the phone is engaged,** messages can be recorded on voicemail.
   c **In order to avoid damage to the machine,** stones must be removed from fruit.
   d Contact your local dealer **if you have problems with your new television.**
   e **As the door closes,** the light inside the refrigerator goes off.
   f **In order to keep a DVD in good condition,** it should be kept in its case.
   g **When someone leaves a message on the answering machine,** a number appears in the display panel.
   h The juice is separated from the pulp **as the fruit is pushed into the feed tube.**

Unit 2 B

1 **a** As air is drawn into the dryer
   b in order to avoid electrocution
   c if you want maximum heat
   d As you move the dryer over your hair
   e when your hair is dry

2 **a** is used for
   b consists of
   c and so
   d are reflected
   e If

   f is placed
   g begins
   h In order to
   i must be turned
   j When
   k avoid

3 *Suggested order*:
   2–f, 3–b, 4–g, 5–e, 6–d, 7–a, 8–h, 9–c.

4 Students' own answers

5 Students' own answers

6 Students' own answers

7 Students' own answers

8 **W**ater-wheels are a very old form of water power**.** They can be **made** of wood or metal. They are found in many **countries** of the world. There are 17 wooden water-wheels, called 'nurias', in the city of Hama in **S**yria. Water-wheels are **usually** located on fast-flowing **rivers** or streams. **A**s the river flows**,** the wheel is turned by the power of the water. The power **is** used to take **water** from the river for farming**.**

9 A computer **(it)** is a very powerful instrument. Some computers are heavy and **are** placed on desks. Other computers are quite small and can **be** carried in the pocket. A computer **has** many different uses. Information **is** given to the computer and a set of instructions, called a programme. The computer is **told** what to do by the programme. A computer **(is)** consists of a monitor with a screen, a keyboard, a disk drive, speakers and a mouse. The keyboard and the mouse are **used** for getting information into the computer. The 'output' **(it)** is shown on **a** computer screen.

10 **A** switch off **B** cut **C** push **D** wait
   E listen **F** remove **G** press **H** lift

11 **A** monitor **B** keyboard **C** screen
   D printer/scanner **E** mouse

Unit 2 Language review

1 **a** The TV channel can be changed with the remote control.
   b The vegetables are cooked in the steamer.
   c My mobile can be used to download music.
   d The European and Asian sides of Istanbul are connected by bridges.
   e The lift must not be used when there is a fire.
   f A satnav is used to give directions.

2 Students' own answers

3 **a** Digital photos can be transferred to a computer and sorted into groups.
   b The ice trays are filled with water and placed carefully into the freezer compartment.
   c Cars are washed by machine at the carwash, dried with hot air and polished by hand.

4   a As you leave the room, please switch off the lights.
    b As global warming increases, the sea level may rise.
    c As the heart beats, blood is pumped around the body.
    d Water is extracted from the clothes as the dryer spins.
    e Electricity is produced as the wind turns the blades of the wind turbine.
    f Food will probably become more expensive as the population of the world increases.

5   Students' own answers

6   a If the camera stops working, check that the battery is fully charged.
    b If there is an earthquake, everyone must leave the building immediately.
    c If your car breaks down on the road, call the emergency number.
    d The amount of water must be increased if the plants start to die.
    e Try moving to another part of your house if you have no signal on your mobile.
    f Their heart rate should decrease if people exercise every day.

7   Students' own answers

8   a Avoid strong sunlight in order to get the best pictures.
    b Shut down your computer at night in order to save electricity.
    c Clean the juice extractor carefully after use in order to avoid blockages.
    d Cars should be polished regularly in order to protect the paintwork.
    e A mobile phone operator must have a good network in order to provide a strong signal for its users.
    f Exercise, rest and a good diet are required in order to keep the body healthy.
    g Important messages should be saved in order to listen to them again.

9   Students' own answers

Unit 3 A

1   1 E (soaked) 2 F (drained) 3 B (steamed)
    4 D (mixed) 5 C (poured) 6 A (served)

2   are placed, are covered, is added, are steamed, are drained, is kept, should be kept, are put, is formed, are mixed, are added, is squeezed, is added, is poured, is added, are placed, can be added, is served

3   See Q.2 answers

4   Then, then, meanwhile, After that, Finally

5   a First of all, Then, then, After that, then, Lastly
    b **is**: named, marked, put, opened. **are**: used, made, filled. **modal**: be laid, be painted, be added, be used
    c To choose the best route.
    d surveyors

e When the route is ready
f Road markings and road signs

6   1 E, 2 D, 3 B, 4 F, 5 C, 6 A

7   a by heating a mixture of flowers and water.
    b by squeezing the cheesecloth.
    c by reducing the quantity.

8   Students' own answers

9   a Hummus is made by mixing chickpeas and tahini paste together.
    b A message is recorded by speaking into the microphone.
    c Drivers are protected by wearing their seatbelts.
    d The liquid in the saucepan is concentrated by heating.
    e An eReader can be charged by connecting it to a computer.

10 a boiling in a pan of water.
    b throwing the dice.
    c pressing a button.
    d mixing yellow and blue.
    e By using the remote control, the channels can be changed.
    f By mixing red and white, pink is produced.
    g By studying hard, a new language can be learned.

    Also comes after the verb *to be* (*is*) and modals (*can*). It comes before the main verb.

11 a They also grow naturally in the Amazon region of Brazil.
    b It can also be moved by clicking the mouse.
    c She also does a lot of important work for the United Nations.
    d They are also an important source of water for some villages.
    e The cover should also be closed to keep dust from the screen.

12 a She also likes reading novels.
    b It is also the capital of China.
    c It also flies to the US.
    d They are also grown in the Far East.
    e It is also used to produce petrol.
    f However, we can also read the news online.

13 a Kuala Lumpur, which is the capital of Malaysia, is located in the west of the country.
    b The Spanish dish paella, which is popular with both Spaniards and tourists, consists mainly of rice and seafood.
    c Gold is mined in South Africa which has the largest gold deposits in the world.
    d Cashew nuts are grown in Kerala which is a beautiful state in the south of India.

14 a which is very useful for luggage, which is strange
    b which are white in colour

c which is situated on the top of tall buildings or hills, which cover the whole area

d which is named after a poem, which are over 1500m in places, which of course increases the cost of the project, which consists of concrete or asphalt, which is cloth with very small holes in it
Total = 10

15 There are two possible ways of joining each pair of sentences.

a Kuwait, which is situated in the north of the Gulf, has a population of more than one million. Kuwait, which has a population of more than one million, is situated in the north of the Gulf.

b Bananas, which are grown in tropical countries such as the Philippines, need a hot, humid climate.

c The King Faisal Causeway, which connects Saudi Arabia and Bahrain, is 24 miles long.

d A scanner, which is an important part of a modern office, works by making a digital copy of a document.

e The rababa, which is a kind of one-string violin, is made of goat skin stretched over a wooden frame.

16 a An answering machine records messages, which can then be played back when you get home.

b My brother has just bought a Land Rover, which is one of the most popular four-wheel-drive vehicles in the Gulf.

c Last week we visited Petra, which is the most famous historical site in Jordan.

d The surface of the road is then sprayed with asphalt, which is a dark, sticky substance produced from petroleum.

e Strips of rubber are passed through rollers, which flatten the strips and produce thin sheets.

17 a although I have to switch it off at college when I'm in class, although it's second-hand

b although it is rather expensive to buy in shops

18 a Although fishermen have the money to buy modern boats, they often prefer to use the old wooden ones.

b Although the car is eight years old, it is in excellent condition.

c Although Egypt has very low rainfall, many crops can be grown using irrigation.

d Although the computer is quite powerful, the modem is rather slow.

e Although it can be very cold in Hong Kong in the winter, it never snows.

f Although those watches are very cheap, they are also very attractive.

g Although some perfumes are made in India, most are imported from France.

19 Students' own answers

20 a Although the suitcase is very large, it only weighs 6kg.

b Baghdad, which is the capital of Iraq, is situated on the River Tigris.

c Jemila sends email messages all the time, although she found computers difficult to use at first.

d Last summer we flew to Singapore on Qantas, which is an Australian airline.

e Although Toyota is a Japanese company, Toyota cars are built in many different countries.

f The Dubai shopping festival, which takes place in March every year, attracts thousands of visitors from all over the region.

g A juice extractor can be used for most types of fruit and vegetables, although it is not very suitable for oranges and lemons.

Unit 3 B

1 a **1** First of all   **2** also   **3** Then
    4 Meanwhile,   **5** also,   **6** Finally,
b After, 'blinis' in Line 1
c After 'caviar' at the end

2 a which   b Although   c As   d When
e in order to   f If   g which   h until

3 Students' own answers

4 Students' own answers

5 Students' own answers

6 grow = grown, will be ready = is ready, are (line 6) = is, usually it is picked = is usually picked, collect = collected, separating = separated, send = sent, are = is

7 *Paradise Restaurant*

Do you like delicious, spicy food **served** in beautiful surroundings? Yes? Then visit our new 'Paradise Restaurant'. We are **located** Ocean Avenue in the centre of the city. Our restaurant, which has wonderful views of the city, is on the **tenth** floor of the Toyota Tower. The menu, **which** is prepared by our experienced chef, contains Chinese, Malaysian and Indonesian dishes. Although our prices are low, you will find that the quality of the food is very **high**. Come and visit us soon!

8

	a bridge	a well	the foundations	a plan	a hole	an omelette
build	✓	✓	✓	✗	✗	✗
draw up	✗	✗	✗	✓	✗	✗
lay	✗	✗	✓	✗	✗	✗
construct	✓	✓	✓	✓	✗	✗
make	✓	✓	✓	✓	✓	✓
drill	✗	✓	✗	✗	✓	✗
dig	✗	✓	✓	✗	✓	✗

9 **A** boil **B** drain **C** cover **D** steam
   E measure **F** heat **G** mix **H** pour **I** add

10 **A** cut **B** collect **C** spread **D** pour into **E** plant
    F transport **G** pick **H** export **I** pass through

Unit 3 Language review

1 **a** cut **b** made **c** dug **d** laid **e** built
   f sent **g** taken **h** drawn **i** seen **j** found

2 The population of many areas of the world is growing
   rapidly. As a result there is a great need for new
   towns. One example is Shatin in the Hong Kong
   region of China. New towns such as Shatin **are** usually
   built in rural areas. Before construction can begin,
   the land **is mapped** by surveyors. Aerial and satellite
   photos **are** also **needed**. The architects, planners and
   engineers look at the maps and plans **are drawn** up
   for the new town. When everyone has agreed on
   the plans, work can begin. First of all, roads **are laid**.
   Electric power and water **are brought** to the site
   and drains **are dug**. Then buildings, such as houses,
   apartment blocks, schools and shops **are constructed**.
   Finally, trees and gardens **are planted** in order to make
   the town more attractive.

3 **a** cooks **b** surgeons **c** mechanics
   d announcers **e** architects **f** everyone

4 Students' own answers

5 **a** It is also used by many older people.
   b He also works in a restaurant in the evenings.
   c It may also be sent by email.
   d They are also found in the mountains of Oman.
   e They can also book hotels if required.
   f Some supermarkets also sell clothes.

6 e – d – c – a – b

7 Students' own answers

8 **a** Tariq felt tired although it was only nine o'clock and
      decided to go to bed.
   b Maria didn't go to university although she became
      a successful businesswoman.
   c Many Indians love to buy gold although it is very
      expensive at the moment.
   d Hummus is available in supermarkets although
      many people prefer to make it at home.
   e Sue studied Cantonese for three years although she
      can't speak it very well.

9 Students' own answers

Unit 4 A

1 Picture B

2 *Regular*: replied, opened, looked, used, explained
   Irregular: left, were, was, said, forgot

3 decided, left, found, had, continued, began,
   appeared, started, were, became, was

4 was beginning, was getting, were beginning

5 had used, hadn't seen

6 **b** In an apartment not far from downtown Miami.
   c Because she hadn't seen her for six years.
   d Because her husband got a job there.
   e Because she lived in the same building.

7 said, explained; told, explained

8 **a** told **b** explained **c** asked, replied **d** said

9 *Picture 1*: 'The engine's on fire!'
   Picture 2: 'We are going to land in the sea.'
   Picture 3: 'Put on your life jackets.'

10 **a** many = many of the passengers,
       some = some of the passengers
    b he = the pilot, us = the passengers
    c there = the emergency exit
    d their = International Air's

11 **b** past perfect
    c past perfect
    d past continuous
    e could, would

12 live/lived, borrowed/had borrowed, never run out/
    had never run out, 's starting/was starting, can't/
    couldn't, will phone/would phone

13 **a** The teacher said that the class was cancelled.
    b Miriam told us that she would be late.
    c The pilot said that there was a problem with
       the engine.
    d The policeman told me to drive more carefully.
    e Faisal said that his cousin had used the car
       last week.

14 **a** Zainab said that she was not feeling well.
    b Our teacher told us that the examinations would
       be on 23rd May.
    c The man said that he had lost his passport. (The
       man told the immigration officer that he had lost
       his passport.)
    d Abdullah said that he had been there the
       previous week.
    e The woman said she came from Shanghai.
    f The young man said he couldn't do a bungee jump.

15 **a** After a large lunch, John fell asleep for twenty
       minutes.
    b Before starting the boat, make sure you check that
       there is enough petrol.
    c After living in Rome for six years, we moved to
       Istanbul.
    d Before buying the dress, Nina tried it on.
    e After writing the letter, Mike faxed it to the head
       office in Cairo.
    f Before travelling to China, Ibn Battuta visited
       Mecca.

16 a Ronaldo, who is an excellent football player, scored six goals last week.

b I've just had a phone call from my sister, who is studying at a college in Manila.

c The mechanic, who was very experienced, said he could repair the car by the following day.

d This morning I went to see the doctor, who said I should rest for three days.

e Mohsin is reading a book about Atatürk, who was the founder of modern Turkey.

f Our English teacher, who is very kind, hard-working and helpful, is probably the best teacher in the college.

17 Students' own answers

18 a The Pathans, who come from the mountainous regions of Pakistan, speak Pashto as their mother tongue.

b Anna, who has just graduated from the University of Singapore, wants to be an economist.

c The Druze are a religious sect, who live mainly in the mountainous regions of Lebanon and southern Syria.

d My uncle, who doesn't speak a word of English, told me that he is planning to visit America in the summer.

e Yesterday I went to visit my grandmother, who is in hospital with a chest complaint.

f Italians, who are well known for their love of music, have some of the world's greatest opera singers.

19 a After walking for six miles in the hot sun, the man finally found a garage.

b Before cooking the sardines, they washed them and cut them into pieces.

c After landing in the sea and waiting for the rescue boats, the passengers finally escaped.

d Before going on a boat trip, make sure that there is petrol in the spare can.

20 a 'I'd like a single room,' he told the receptionist.

b 'What's the time?' Carlos asked. 'Six o'clock,' I replied.

c 'Follow the London Road and turn left at the roundabout,' explained Tania.

d 'It's very hot today,' said Boris. 'I think I'll go for a swim.'

Unit 4 B

1 1e, 2b, 3h, 4d, 5a, 6f, 7g, 8c:

On Saturday, Gabriella who is a very close friend of mine, invited me to her house. She was having a small party for her daughter, Elena. My father, who doesn't work on Saturdays, offered to take me in his car and I arrived about two o'clock. The house, which was quite large, was full of people. There was a lot of noise from the children, who were playing with a plastic beach ball. Gabriella asked me if I wanted to meet Elena's teacher. I said 'Yes,' and so she took me into the garden and I was introduced to Koula who was sitting under a tree. Gabriella brought us both some orange juice and a huge chocolate cake, which she had baked for Elena's party. I want to be a teacher too and so I asked Koula many questions about teaching. She told me that she had studied at a teacher training college in Thessaloniki, which is a large city in the north east of Greece. After leaving college, she went to teach in a small village school. Three years ago she moved to Athens and started teaching at Elena's school, which is only half a kilometre from her home. I asked her what she liked most about teaching. 'The children,' she replied. 'They are lovely.' At that moment, the ball landed on the table and knocked the cake and orange juice onto the ground. 'Well, I like them most of the time,' she added with a smile.

2 A b ate **c** were becoming **d** saw **e** picked **f** up **g** was **h** jumped out
B j said **k** explained **l** had rescued **m** could ask **n** asked **o** replied
C q asked **r** was **s** told **t** clapped **u** disappeared **v** bring

3 Students' own answers

4 a who **b** that **c** although **d** in order to **e** which **f** After **g** before **h** if **i** who **j** when

5 Students' own answers

6 Students' own answers

7 Students' own answers

8 Students' own answers

9 Students' own answers

10 One day last summer, my family went for a **picnic** in a park near the sea. We **left** home early in the morning and found a quiet place under some trees. We put up the tent, which we always take with us, and my sister and I began to prepare some food. After eating, we **were** all resting near the **tent** and Somboon, **who** is my youngest son, was playing with a ball. I told him to go and **play** near the trees. A few minutes later, he screamed and fell to the ground. We all ran over and found him holding his **foot**. 'What's the matter?' I **asked**. 'It's my foot,' he cried. 'Something bit me.' Then we **saw** a large scorpion in the grass. I told my husband to kill it quickly. He picked up a stick and hit it hard until it was no longer moving. Then he said he would take **S**omboon to the hospital. We all went with him in the jeep. I was very **worried** because Somboon was breathing with difficulty.

11 a said **b** explained **c** told **d** asked **e** added **f** replied

12 *worried*: nervous, afraid, frightened, concerned, anxious, tense

calm: relaxed, tranquil, peaceful, quiet, still

13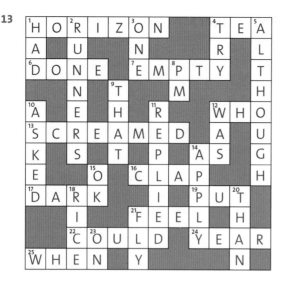

Unit 4 Language review

1 **a** owned **b** grew **c** knew **d** decided
   e were **f** had **g** put **h** was
   i sank **j** died **k** survived **l** was able to swim
   m climbed **n** had **o** found **p** shared

2 **a** was, was sleeping, were watching
   b fell, arrived
   c rained, drove, braked, couldn't stop, crashed
   d came, were looking, found

3 **a** I had eaten earlier
   b had not rained for six months
   c he had studied it at school for six years
   d had worked very hard
   e he had moved to Australia

4 **a** Lee said that he would give you the money later.
   b Andy said he was studying Engineering at MRT University.
   c Hari said he didn't speak Malay, but he could read it.
   d Dr Hussain said the treatment had been successful.
   e Stefani said he worked in a clothing factory but he was looking for another job.

5 **a** said **b** told **c** told **d** said **e** told **f** said

6 **a** After fully charging the battery, the phone is ready to use.
   b Before placing the eggs in the pan, make sure the water is boiling.
   c After you complete the form, send it to the address at the top of the page.
   d Before the robbers entered the bank, they put on dark glasses.
   e Before buying a new mobile, Sonia checked several websites to compare prices.

7 **a** My brother, who is a pilot for British Airways, flies all over the world.
   b I enjoyed watching Usain Bolt, who is the world's fastest runner, during the Olympics.
   c Yesterday, I met our new professor who will teach us Physics next semester.

   d Last night, I was chatting with a close friend who lives in Indonesia.

8 Students' own answers

Unit 5 A

1 To either study in Exeter or Edinburgh

2 **For:** lovely city, good climate, warmer in winter, less windy
   Against: smaller than Edinburgh, less interesting, long way from family, more expensive, pay for accommodation

3 Exeter.
   a She must take the course which is best.
   b Fly home to Edinburgh if there is a flight from Exeter.
   c Try to talk to a friend or a member of the family.

4 **a** colder **b** more interesting **c** heavier
   d more useful **e** larger **f** faster **g** more beautiful

5 better than, smaller than, less windy, less interesting, more expensive, less expensive, more comfortable, the best, the coldest, the quickest, the most suitable, the most important

6 **a** the tallest **b** the most popular
   c the most famous **d** the biggest
   e the closest **f** the most productive

7 **a** books, **b** eReader

8 Sam: books – easier to use
                    – more enjoyable
                    – less convenient for travelling
   Yoko: eReaders – easier to use
                      – more enjoyable
          books – less convenient for travelling

9 Students' own answers

10 Students' own answers

11 **a** Rome – has – hotter summers – than – London.
    b Fresh fruit juice – is – healthier – than – cola.
    c Coconut palms – are – much taller – than – date palms.
    d A boiled egg – is – easier to prepare – than – an omelette.

12 **a** Chinese – is – more – difficult – to learn – than – English.
    b Business letters – are – less – personal – than – email messages.
    c An ordinary mobile– is – less – useful – than – a smartphone.
    d Gold – is – much more – expensive – to buy – than – silver.

13 **a** Victor is more intelligent than Ernesto.
    b Watermelons are cheaper than pineapples.
    c Istanbul is more beautiful than Ankara.
    d Koshiba is better than Toni.
    e A mobile phone is quicker than rescue flares.

14 **b Defining:** which has the most suitable course, that I really want to do, which sometimes seems like the coldest place in the world, which is the best for you, that you will make, that I don't know, that you want
Non-defining: which I downloaded from Amazon, which I could go to in Edinburgh

15 **a** On our trip to India last year the place <u>which I liked best</u> was Darjeeling.
b Yesterday in the supermarket I saw the woman <u>who reads the news on Channel 33</u>.
c The exam <u>which was planned for tomorrow</u> has been postponed until next week.
d This is the car <u>that I want to buy</u>.
e The wadi <u>that we visited for the field trip</u> was one of the most interesting in Oman
f People <u>who study rocks</u> are called geologists.

16 **a** That's the man that I saw earlier today.
b We went to see the film which won all the Oscars and we liked it.
c The car that I would really like to buy is a bit too expensive.
d The waitress who we gave our order to has disappeared.
e The country which has the biggest population is China.
f The college presents a prize to the student that gets the best exam results.
g The topic that I would like to discuss in this lecture is climate change.

17 *Possible answers*:
a ... hit my car
b ... that I bought last week
c ... which I liked most on our trip last year
d ... who/that go to football matches

18 **a** who is an expert in economics
b Students' own answers

19 **a** Canberra, which is the capital of Australia, is not the biggest city in the country.
b The shop had sold out of Jasmine Mystery, which is my favourite perfume.
c The man who robbed the bank was arrested yesterday.
d The main course was sardines, which are popular in Portugal.
e Last week I wrote a letter to the college that I want to study in.
f Yu Lin said she wanted to speak to the woman who was in charge of the shop.
g The programme that I wanted to watch was cancelled at the last minute.
h Peter, who is a well-known journalist, writes for a Cape Town newspaper.
i All appointments have been cancelled by the president, who has a slight stomach upset.

Unit 5 B

1 **a** On the one hand, **b** But **c** when
d less **e** which **f** However **g** more
h who **i** whereas **j** Although

2 Sources of energy in an increasing populated world.

3 Paragraph A – b, e, d, c, a.
Paragraph B – h, i, g, k, f, l, j.

4 Students' own answers.

5 **a** the general reader   **b** formal
c a friend (Aunt Sarah)   **d** informal

6 **a** advertisement
b very interesting
c send me
d I am
e would like to find
f quite well
g a little
h a great deal
i very
j I have
k you wish
l I look forward to hearing from you
m Yours faithfully

7 Students' own answers

8 Students' own answers

9 Students' own answers

10 Students' own answers

11 There are two buildings which (**they**) are **suitable** for the company. One is a building called Panorama House. It **is** located close to the city centre in Station Road. The total area is 1,350sq m. It has six floors and a small reception area. **There** are six toilets and a small kitchen. From the sixth floor there are **lovely** views of the city. The second possibility is a **building** called Park Mansions, which (**it**) is much larger **than** Panorama House. It has eight **floors**. The reception area is **bigger** too, **which** (**it**) is very important for the company. Unfortunately the rent is more **expensive** than the rent for Panorama House. It is $6,000 per month, **whereas** the rent for Panorama House is only $5,000. The location is less convenient too. Panorama House is (**more**) closer to the city centre.

12 *Suggested answer*:

There are **many** different types of plants, **for example** ferns, conifers and angiosperms. The largest group of plants are angiosperms, which **are also called** flowering plants. Flowering plants produce flowers which produce seeds and fruit. (**Well,**) Flowering plants can be divided into two more types.

These are called monocots and dicots. The monocot, which means 'one seed-leaf' (**by the way**), has (**got**) long narrow leaves. The veins in the leaves are all **parallel**. An example of **a monocot** is the palm tree. On the other hand, the dicot (**i.e.** 'two seeded-leaf') has broader leaves. The veins are **also** different. There **is** a main vein and (**then**) there are **smaller** veins branching off. A tomato plant is an example of a dicot. These two types of angiosperm **can be seen** in the **photos**.

13 hot – hotter – hottest; big – bigger – biggest; wet – wetter – wettest; nice – nicer – nicest; heavy – heavier – heaviest; dry – drier – driest; easy – easier – easiest

14 good – better – the best; bad – worse – the worst; much/many – more – the most; little – less – the least; old – older– the oldest

15 a Baikal – deepest
b longest – Nile
c Indonesia – greatest (largest)
d highest – Venezuela
e coldest – Antarctica
f Al Azziziyah – hottest

16 a suitable
b comfortable
c pleasant
d personal
e interesting
f difficult
g reliable
h exciting
i intelligent
Vertical word = important.

Unit 5 Language review

1 a Travelling by plane is better than travelling by car.
b Writing on a keyboard is easier than with a pen.
c Chinese is more difficult to learn than French.
d Petrol is much more expensive in Germany than in Saudi Arabia.
e My Internet connection at home is slower than the connection at work.
f I think that football is a more exciting game than cricket.
g Studying at home would be less interesting than studying at an overseas university.

2 Students' own answers

3 a The best silk in the world is made in China.
b The most expensive metal is gold.
c My most exciting holiday was when we went to India.
d Some people say that Vancouver has the worst climate.
e One of the most interesting places to visit in China is the Forbidden City.
f This is the least reliable car I have owned.
g Walking is often the quickest way to get around in a city.

4 Students' own answers

5 a The film which I enjoyed most last year was …
b The person in the world that I admire most is …
c … is the country that I would most like to visit …

6 a This country, which is one of the largest in the world, is situated in South America.
b The capital, which is not the biggest city, is located in the middle of the country.
c The people, who speak mainly Portuguese, are famous for their love of football and music. The country is Brazil.

7 a The hospital that we visited was the oldest in the country.
b The car which I bought last week, broke down on the motorway.
c The lecturer said he liked the report that I wrote on the use of the Internet.
d The police are looking for a man who was seen standing outside a bank.
e The actor who played the part of the king in the TV series, died suddenly last week.

8 a Usain Bolt, who is a famous Jamaican sprinter, is one of the most respected men in his sport.
b The jeep, which has a roof rack and an extra petrol tank, is perfect for trips across the desert.
c More than 400 students are expected to enrol at the New International University, which is opening next month.
d Bill Gates, who is one of the richest men in the world, has decided to give most of his money to charity.
e Sri Lanka, which is an island located in the Indian Ocean, lies to the south of India.

Unit 6 A

1 a

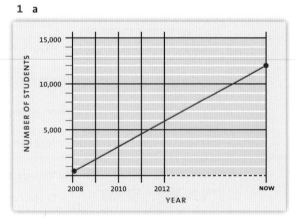

2 b They came from the area around Riyadh.
c From all over Saudi Arabia.
d Because there were no trees or gardens.
e Because there are gardens and fountains.

3 **a** have been studying, was opened, has grown, has increased, has become. Total = 5

b since it was opened

c 3

d it used to be very dry and dusty

4 **a** **C** mainframe computer

B silicon chip

E the desktop

A laptop

D the tablet

b For the last fifty years, computers have been getting faster, cheaper and smaller. They have also become more powerful.

5 **a** they = computers; one = a computer; this = the invention of the silicon chip; it = the Osbourne 1; then = 1981

b a = of calculations; b = which was; c = of computers; d = which were

6

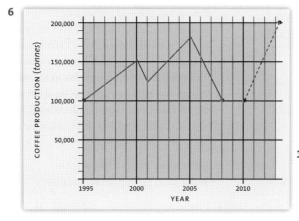

7 **a** 3 **b** 3 **c** 1 **d** 3 **e** 2 **f** 1

8 Students' own answers

9 **a** Maha has been working in a bank since 2011.

b The boys have been washing their car since six o'clock.

c I have known Sarah since she was a little girl.

d My family has kept horses for many years.

e Ali has been waiting for a bus for twenty minutes.

f People have grown rice in the valley for centuries.

10 Students' own answers

11 Students' own answers

12 There are two possible ways of joining each sentence as shown in **1**.

1 Keiko is studying Business Studies, English and Computing because he wants to work for a large multinational company. or Because he wants to work for a large multinational company, Keiko is studying Business Studies, English and Computing.

2 Coffee production fell dramatically last year because many trees were destroyed by bad weather.

3 More and more people are buying computers because they are becoming cheaper and cheaper.

4 Nina couldn't come to the birthday party yesterday because she was taking an examination at the college.

5 The government is building ten new schools because the population of the country has been increasing rapidly in recent years.

6 Boris has been trying to save money for the last six months because he wants to go on holiday to San Francisco in the summer.

13 Students' own answers

14 **a** Because of this, coffee production fell sharply that year to 120,000 tonnes. As a result, many trees had to be destroyed in order to stop over-production of coffee.

15 When the business started, (f) there was just one office and three employees.

As the machine spins around, (b) the juice is extracted from the fruit.

In order to increase coffee production, (d) many new trees had to be planted.

If there is WiFi in a coffee shop, (e) you can connect your smartphone to the Internet.

Although the weather was bad, (c) we decided to make the trip to Fujaira.

Because the weather was bad, (a) we decided to cancel the trip to Fujaira.

16 *Possible answers*:

a is from Beirut,

b are located just outside Cairo,

c was president of South Africa,

d is studying at a university in Washington.

e is a beautiful city in the north-west of Turkey.

f is a popular dish in the Arab world,

17 **a** The man wearing a brown jacket is a chemistry professor.

b The tall tower built like a rocket is the Holiday Hotel.

c The president is the short, fat man speaking to the old lady.

d The country most famous for growing coffee is Brazil.

e Andrea Bocelli is a blind Italian singer known for his wonderful voice.

18 **A**eroplanes have been getting bigger and faster over the years. **T**he first modern aeroplane was the **B**oeing 247, which was introduced in 1933. **I**t had room for 10 passengers. **D**uring the **S**econd **W**orld **W**ar the jet engine was developed. **T**he first jet airliner, which was called the **C**omet, started service in 1952. **I**t had four jet engines and could fly at 885kph. **L**ater, in 1958, **P**an **A**merican **A**irlines introduced the **B**oeing 707, which could carry 112 passengers. **B**ecause of the powerful engines, the plane was able to cross the **A**tlantic from **N**ew **Y**ork to **L**ondon in less than eight hours, which was half the time of the old propeller aircraft.

Unit 6 B

1 **a** informal

b from my bed, bit by bit, I can't wait

c Dear Mrs Fernandez,

I'm writing this letter to you from my bed. I broke my leg badly three weeks ago on the stairs in the university. I was in a hurry because I was late for class. As I was running down the stairs from the first floor to the ground floor, I slipped and fell to the bottom. I felt a terrible pain in my left leg and I couldn't move. At the hospital the doctor, who is a friend of my father's, told me that my leg was broken. After resetting my leg in plaster, he said that I should rest at home for at least a month and then come back to see him. He told me to phone him if I needed help. Since then I've been at home, which has been rather boring. I've been getting better bit by bit. I've been reading my course books and surfing the Internet, but I can't wait until I can walk again. Sometimes I sit in the garden, which is just outside my bedroom window, if it's not too hot. My older sister, who's not working at the moment, has been looking after me. She's been wonderful!

I'm sorry I am missing your classes. I'll let you know when I can return to the university.

Best wishes,

Sarah

2 g – e – c – h – b – f – a – d

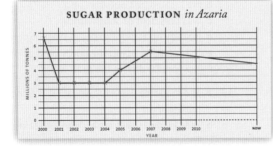

3 **a** but **b** Because of this **c** However

d which **e** also **f** Since **g** Whereas

h which **i** Because **j** Although

4 Students' own answers

5 Students' own answers

6 Students' own answers

7 Students' own answers

8 **a** Global warming is caused by an **increase** in the amount of carbon dioxide in the Earth's atmosphere. Carbon dioxide **is** produced naturally by vegetation. It is **an** important part of the atmosphere. It traps the sun's heat. It warms the surface of the Earth. Normally there is a balance between the gases in the atmosphere. In recent years the amount of carbon dioxide has **gone** up. This is because of the burning of fossil fuels and the destruction of forests. The temperature of the Earth's surface **has** been going up. **This** has meant changes in **the** Earth's climate. Many parts of the world are becoming **hotter** and drier. Other parts are experiencing more storms and rainfall. Sea level **(it)** has also been **rising**. This is because the polar ice-caps have been melting.

c Suggested improvement:

Global warming is caused by an increase in the amount of carbon dioxide in the Earth's atmosphere. Carbon dioxide, which is produced naturally by vegetation, is an important part of the atmosphere. It traps the sun's heat and as a result warms the surface of the Earth. Normally there is a balance between the gases in the atmosphere. In recent years, however, the amount of carbon dioxide has gone up because of the burning of fossil fuels and the destruction of forests. As a result the temperature of the Earth's surface has been going up, which has meant changes in the Earth's climate. Many parts of the world are becoming hotter and drier, while other parts are experiencing more storms and rainfall. Sea level has also been rising. This is because the polar ice-caps have been melting.

9 *increase*: grow, go up, improve, rise

decrease: drop, go down, fall, collapse

10 **a** Chemistry **b** Physics **c** Biology **d** History

e Geography **f** Mathematics **g** Computer Science

11 **a** Science **b** Law **c** Education

d Arts **e** Engineering

12

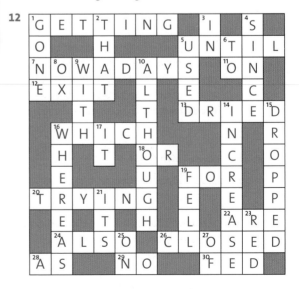

Unit 6 Language review

1 **a** The population of Abu Dhabi has increased dramatically since 1970.
  b There has been a big rise in the number of cars.
  c People have come from all over the world to live in Abu Dhabi.
  d The government has built many new schools and hospitals for the growing population.
  e The oil and gas industries have grown rapidly since 1970.
  f Many large companies have set up offices in Abu Dhabi.
  g Tourism has gone up sharply during this period.
  h Many new roads and bridges have been built in recent years.

2 **a** Lee has been working in an electronics company for six years.
  b My little brother has been playing computer games all day.
  c I have been learning to play the piano since I was little.
  d The price of gold has been falling recently.
  e We have been living in America since 2005.
  f How long have you been studying at the university?
  g My grandfather has been driving for 40 years and he has never had an accident.
  h I'm sorry I'm late. Have you been waiting long?

3 **a** Professor Lee has worked in the same university for twenty years.
  b Maria has been talking on the phone for nearly two hours.
  c Kuala Lumpur has grown rapidly in recent years.
  d The chicken has been roasting in the oven since ten o'clock.
  e How long have your relatives been living in China?
  f Tony has studied French since he moved to Paris.

4 Students' own answers

5 **a** The team's best player was sick last week. As a result, they played badly and lost an important match.
  b Hari's computer broke down last week. Because of this, he was unable to hand in the assignment on time.
  c The government has increased the price of petrol. As a result, motorists are feeling very upset.
  d The building started to shake a few hours ago. Because of this, many people ran out into the street.
  e It has been raining since early this morning. As a result, this afternoon's cricket match has been cancelled.
  f The price of laptops has been falling over the last few years. Because of this, more and more people can afford to buy them.

6 **a** The doctor treating my father is very well qualified.
  b Yesterday we went to the Chinese restaurant mentioned in all the guide books.
  c The factory closed down last winter will reopen next month.
  d Each year the teacher voted the best by all the students is given a prize by the headmaster.
  e The person I admire the most in all the world is Barack Obama.
  f The computer I want to buy is too expensive for me at the moment.

7 **a** Although the climb was very difficult in places, we managed to reach the top of the mountain before midday.
  b The course in architecture had to be cancelled, because there weren't enough students.
  c When I first saw the university campus, I knew I would be happy studying there.
  d Sales usually fall as the price of a product rises.
  e The new director of the college, who comes from Toulouse in south-west France, called a meeting for all the staff.
  f The survey, which we carried out last semester, showed that most students preferred to study at home and not in the library.
  g The car that my brother bought had to go to the garage after just one week.
  h If I had as much money as Bill Gates, I would also give it to charity.